FATHERHOOD

by design

FATHERHOOD *by design*

A Father's Guide to Intentional Leadership and Lasting Influence

ERIK WESTRUM

ISBNs: Ebook: 978-1-967732-03-6

Paperback: 978-1-967732-04-3

Hardcover: 978-1-967732-05-0

START STRONG WITH YOUR FREE GIFT!

Before you dive in, I want to give you something to *kickstart your journey.*

Join the FREE 7-Day "Fatherhood by Design" Challenge—a powerful, purpose-filled experience designed to help you become more present, intentional, and influential as a father and leader.

Visit www.erikwestrumbook.com to get your free gift today Or scan the QR code to access it instantly!

This challenge will help you take immediate action on the principles you're about to learn—because growth starts with *doing*, not just reading.

Let's go!

DAD

You've always been my hero.
Thank you for showing up, for loving me unconditionally,
and for being the kind of father I aspire to be.
Love you always — Erik

DEDICATION

To my incredible wife, Kelly—your unconditional love, patience, and support make me a better man, husband, and father every single day. Thank you for believing in me, standing beside me, and reminding me of what truly matters.

To my amazing children—Luke, Ethan, Isabella, and Evelina—you are my greatest joy, my daily inspiration, and the reason I strive to be a better father. Each of you has shaped me in ways I never imagined, and I am endlessly grateful for the privilege of being your dad.

This book is for you. May it serve as a reminder that fatherhood is not just a role, but a calling—a sacred opportunity to lead, love, and leave a lasting legacy. I pray I show up consistently to help guide you to a life honoring Jesus. Amen.

"But the fruit of the Spirit is love, joy, peace, patience, kindness, goodness, faithfulness, gentleness, and self-control."

– GALATIANS 5:22

TABLE OF CONTENTS

INTRODUCTION

THE FATHER'S CALLING

"Train up a child in the way he should go; even when he is old, he will not depart from it."

– PROVERBS 22:6

Welcome to a journey of transformation and deeper connection with your children. This book is designed to address the profound challenges fathers face in becoming truly present, intentional, and influential in their children's lives. It transcends the principles of fatherhood by providing specific steps to transform those principles into daily practices that encourage discipline, leadership, and meaningful relationships.

WHY THIS BOOK? MY MOTIVATION FOR WRITING IT

Fatherhood is one of the greatest leadership roles a man can have. It is not a title earned simply by bringing a child into the world; it is a responsibility that must be lived out daily. Every decision you make, every word you speak, and every action you take shapes the foundation upon which your children will build their lives.

Yet, too many men fall into the trap of passive fatherhood—present but not engaged, providing but not leading. I've been there myself. The world tells us that as long as we work hard, put food on the table, and show up for the occasional game or activity, we have done our part. But fatherhood is not a spectator sport.

Your presence, discipline, and example are the blueprint your children will follow—for better or worse.

As a former professional athlete, coach, and father of four, I've experienced firsthand the intense pressures and joys of parenting. The strategies and insights I share here are ones I've learned—often through trial and error—and have seen work for others in similar situations.

I've met countless fathers who struggle to balance their careers with the desire to be more involved parents. One father told me how he always felt he was "just in time" or "just good enough," never really mastering the art of being present in the moment with his children. Another shared his fear of not being a strong enough example for his kids. These conversations, and many others like them, deeply influenced the writing of this book. Most importantly, it was my stories of not showing up the way I wanted to that really challenged me to look at myself as a father.

MY WAKE-UP CALL FROM PASSIVE TO PRESENT

I used to believe that being a good dad meant providing. That as long as there was a roof over my family's head, food on the table, and a stable life, I was fulfilling my role. I convinced myself that my presence—simply being in the house, sitting at the dinner table, attending the occasional game or activity—was enough.

And in some seasons, I really was all in. I'd be "Dad of the Year"—coaching teams, helping with school projects, initiating deep conversations, planning adventures, making breakfast on Saturdays, and soaking in every moment with my kids. I felt like I was nailing it.

But then there were the other seasons. The times when work got overwhelming, stress took over, or I simply convinced myself that I had already done enough. That providing was my main role, and if I was in the house, I believed that it should count for something. I sat on the sidelines, nodding along as my kids spoke but never really engaging. I'd get home exhausted, my mind elsewhere, offering absent-minded responses to their stories before scrolling through emails or sports highlights.

It wasn't that I didn't love them. I loved them deeply. But I saw fatherhood as something I could turn on and off. I showed up in bursts of energy, expecting those moments to carry weight in the times I was non-existent. And for a while, I thought it worked.

Until the moment it didn't.

THE LIGHT BULB MOMENT

One night, I came home late after a long day. My son was sitting at the kitchen table, half-heartedly moving food around on his plate. I asked how his day was, expecting the usual, "Fine." But instead, he shrugged and muttered, "You wouldn't get it, Dad."

Something about that hit me harder than I expected.

"What do you mean?" I asked.

He looked up, hesitated, and then said something I'll never forget:

"Sometimes you're here, and it's awesome. Other times, it's like you don't really care."

I opened my mouth to argue, to say, *Of course I care! I work hard because I care! I provide because I care*! But the words caught in my throat. I looked at him—really looked at him—and saw something I had been avoiding.

Disappointment.

Not anger. Not resentment. Just a quiet, resigned disappointment.

And that's when it hit me.

I had been selfish.

I had convinced myself that fatherhood was about me—about my efforts, my sacrifices, my definition of being "present." I thought that showing up when it was convenient, when I had the energy, was enough. I believed that providing financially was the greatest expression of love. But all my son wanted—all my kids ever wanted—was me. Fully engaged. Fully present. Not just physically there but emotionally, mentally, and spiritually invested.

THE SHIFT

That moment didn't change me overnight. But it planted a seed.

I started paying attention—not just to the big moments, but to the small ones. I noticed how my kids' eyes lit up when I asked follow-up questions about their interests. How they lingered longer at the dinner table when I showed genuine curiosity about their lives. How their confidence grew when I encouraged them rather than just instructing them.

I also saw how easy it was to slip back into my own world. To tell myself, *I'll be more involved next week, next month when work slows down*. But fatherhood doesn't wait. Kids don't pause their lives until you're ready to engage.

So, I made a decision. No more fluctuating between "Dad of the Year" and a spectator. No more convincing myself that providing was enough. I committed to showing up—not just when it was convenient, not just when I had the energy, but every single day.

Not because I had to.

Because I wanted to.

Because fatherhood isn't about me.

It's about them.

And the greatest gift I could ever give my kids wasn't the house they lived in, the vacations we took, or the things I bought them.

It was me.

And that is why this book is for the men who refuse to settle for being a part-time father in their homes. It is for fathers who understand that the way they lead their families today will determine the legacy they leave behind.

FROM THE WARRIORS' SUCCESS TO FATHERHOOD

The Golden State Warriors have exemplified the principle behind the quote, "Leader of one, leader of many. If you can't lead one, you can't lead any," by fostering a culture of self-discipline, accountability, and leadership at every level. Their championship success wasn't built only on talent, but on the belief that every player must first lead himself before he can effectively contribute to the team. Head coach Steve Kerr instilled this mindset by encouraging players to take ownership of their preparation, habits, and mindset—emphasizing that leadership isn't reserved for the captains or star players, but is a responsibility shared by all. Players like Steph Curry and Draymond Green embody this philosophy, setting the tone through their relentless work ethic and commitment to team success. By holding themselves accountable first, they inspire their teammates to do the same, creating an environment where leadership is not dictated from the top but cultivated from within.

The same principle applies to fatherhood. Before we can effectively lead our children, we must first lead ourselves—by living with integrity, modeling discipline, and being intentional with our actions. Just as the Warriors thrive by embracing individual leadership within the team, fathers create strong families by setting an example through their own habits, words, and choices. A father who leads himself well—psychologically, physically, spiritually, and emotionally—sets the foundation for his children to follow, shaping a legacy of leadership that extends far beyond the home.

WHY FATHERS MATTER MORE THAN EVER

We live in a time where distractions are everywhere, and true leadership in the home is more important than ever. Children are being shaped by social media, influencers, and outside forces that do not have their best interests at heart. If fathers do not step up and take the lead, the world will gladly take their place. Is that what you want? Neither do I.

Statistics show that children with engaged, present fathers:

- Have higher self-esteem and emotional security.
- Perform better academically.
- Develop stronger resilience in the face of adversity.
- Are less likely to engage in destructive behaviors.

On the flip side, the absence of a father—physically or emotionally—leaves a void that is often filled with insecurity, confusion, and a desperate search for identity.

As a father, you are the standard in your children's lives. They will learn discipline from you. They will learn respect from you. They will learn how to handle success and failure from you. Your role is not just to provide but to prepare—to equip them with the mindset, habits, and character they need to navigate life successfully.

DISCIPLINE: THE FOUNDATION OF IMPACTFUL FATHERHOOD

Many men associate the word "discipline" with punishment. But true discipline is about structure, consistency, and setting expectations that lead to growth. When a father disciplines himself—whether in his faith, his fitness, his work ethic, or his daily habits—he sets the tone for his household.

Children do not learn discipline by being told what to do; they learn it by watching it lived out. A father who prioritizes discipline in his own life naturally instills it in his children. Whether it's waking up early, following through on commitments, or handling adversity with resilience, these lessons become the pillars of a strong, purpose-driven life.

The greatest gift you can give your children is not material wealth—it is the example of a disciplined, purpose-driven life. It shows them what it means to work hard, to stand by their values, to love their family, and to live with integrity.

THE COMMITMENT TO SHOW UP EVERY DAY

Fatherhood is not about being perfect—it is about being present. Your children do not need a flawless father; they need a consistent one.

Showing up doesn't just mean being there physically—it means engaging in the small, daily moments that truly matter:

- Conversations at the dinner table
- Throwing a football in the backyard
- Praying with your children at bedtime
- Teaching them how to handle failure
- Reinforcing the values you want them to carry into adulthood

There will be days when you fall short. There will be moments when you don't have the answers. But fatherhood is not about never failing—it's about never quitting.

YOUR FATHERHOOD CHALLENGE

As you begin this book, I challenge you to take ownership of your role as a father. Stop looking at fatherhood as something that happens to you and start seeing it as the most important leadership mission you will ever have.

The way you lead your children will not only shape their future—it will ripple through generations.

WHAT YOU'LL FIND IN THIS BOOK

In these pages, you will find a structured approach to becoming the father you want to be. This includes:

- Mastering the art of being physically and emotionally available to your children.
- Leading by example through disciplined actions and choices.

- Creating a Fatherhood Game Plan, a personalized framework tailored to your values and the unique needs of your family.

By the time you finish this book, you will have a clear, actionable strategy to lead your family with purpose, instill discipline in your children, and create a legacy that lasts for generations.

As you read through this book, commit to completing the Fatherhood by Design Game Plan exercises at the end of each chapter. You can write your answers in the space below each exercise, in a notebook or journal, or in a file on your phone or computer.

Thank you for trusting me to guide you through this process. Your commitment to improving as a father will not go unnoticed, and I am confident that the strategies and insights in this book will empower you to build stronger, more meaningful relationships with your children.

FINAL THOUGHT: YOUR CHILDREN ARE WATCHING

You are writing your legacy right now.

Your children will remember the habits you model, the love you show, and the consistency with which you lead.

The only question is: What kind of father do you want them to remember?

It's time to lead. Let's begin this journey together.

THE FATHERHOOD *by Design* GAME PLAN

Write down three core values that you want to pass on to your children. These should be the guiding principles that shape your parenting, leadership, and daily interactions with your children.

Keep this list somewhere visible as a reminder of your commitment to raising strong, disciplined, and impactful children.

Because the values you choose to live by today will become the foundation your children stand on tomorrow.

STEP INTO YOUR CALLING AS A FATHER

You weren't meant to father by default—you were made to father by design.
Your leadership matters. Your presence matters. You matter.

Ready to rise to the challenge?

Scan the QR code or visit www.erikwestrumbook.com to claim your FREE 7-Day Fatherhood Challenge and start leading with purpose today.

Your family is waiting. Your legacy starts now.

CHAPTER 1

THE POWER OF PRESENCE

"A father's presence is more powerful than a thousand words. Your children may forget what you say, but they will never forget how you made them feel."

– Unknown

Fatherhood isn't just a role; it's a profound journey that fundamentally transforms a man as he shapes the lives of his children. It's about more than providing and protecting; it's about instilling values, building resilience, and fostering emotional connections that last a lifetime.

In today's fast-paced world, many fathers mistakenly believe that physical presence alone is enough. You work hard, provide for your family, and ensure they have food on the table and a roof over their heads. But fatherhood is about so much more than providing—it's about connection.

Your presence, when fully engaged, shapes your child's confidence, security, and self-worth. Children don't just need a father in the same room; they need a father who is invested—one who listens, teaches, encourages, and walks alongside them. Your presence is either a source of strength and stability or a void they will spend their lives trying to fill.

PHYSICAL PRESENCE VS. EMOTIONAL PRESENCE

A father can be home but absent at the same time.

You may be sitting in the same room as your kids, but if your mind is elsewhere—lost in work emails, distracted by social media, or preoccupied with stress—you're missing valuable opportunities to connect.

True presence means more than just being there; it means being fully engaged in the moment. Your children need to see you looking them in the eyes, laughing with them, asking questions, and listening without distractions. They need to know that, in a world constantly fighting for your attention, they are your priority.

WHY PRESENCE MATTERS

Your level of engagement as a father has a direct and lasting impact on your child's development. Children spell love as T-I-M-E. The time you give them isn't just spent—it's *invested*. Each moment you're present tells them they are valued, safe, and deeply important.

Even just 1% of your day—15 minutes—can make a difference. But let's be honest: that's the floor, not the ceiling. Fifteen minutes is the *bare minimum*, not the ultimate goal. If you're not currently showing up consistently, start there. Build the habit. But don't stop there.

Because your child is your greatest asset. And while so many fathers spend countless hours chasing temporary rewards—career milestones, hobbies, distractions—our love, presence, and influence are what truly last. Your legacy won't be built in boardrooms or on balance sheets—it'll be built in the quiet, consistent moments you share with your kids.

HOW TO BE FULLY PRESENT

Being an engaged father doesn't require extravagant plans or expensive outings. It simply requires intentionality. Here are ways to cultivate presence in your daily life:

1. Be Where Your Feet Are

When you're with your children, be with them.

Put your phone away, close your laptop, and focus on the conversation or activity at hand.

2. Create One-on-One Time

Every child is unique—and they need to *feel* that you see them that way.

In a world where it's easy to lump siblings together or unintentionally favor the child with shared interests, it becomes even more important to carve out intentional, one-on-one time. Whether it's five minutes before bed, a weekly breakfast outing, or a walk around the block—uninterrupted time tells your child: *"I see you. You matter to me. You are not just part of the group—you are valued as an individual."*

This becomes even more critical in blended families, shared custody situations, or households with many children and limited time. One child may naturally connect with you over sports or shared hobbies, while another may feel left out because their interests are wildly different. That difference isn't a barrier—it's an opportunity. When you take the time to step into *their* world, you're not just building connection—you're building trust, identity, and long-term influence.

One-on-one time doesn't have to be long. It just needs to be *intentional.* Because when your child feels truly seen, they stop comparing. They stop wondering if a sibling is the "favorite." They begin to believe they're irreplaceable—and they are.

3. Ask Better Questions

Move beyond "How was your day?" and ask deeper questions like:

- *What was the best part of your day?*
- *What's something you're excited about right now?*
- *What's one thing you want to get better at?*
- *How can I help you feel more supported?*

4. Get Involved in Their World

If your child loves sports, music, or video games, engage with them in those interests. Learn about what excites them and participate—even if it's outside your comfort zone.

5. Establish Traditions & Rituals

Whether it's a bedtime routine, a weekend adventure, or a simple "Dad & Kid" handshake, create small traditions that reinforce connection and consistency.

6. Show Up at the Right Moments

Big life events matter, but so do the small ones. Being at their games, performances, and school events sends a powerful message: "You are important to me."

OVERCOMING THE BARRIERS TO PRESENCE

Many fathers struggle with their presence because of work demands, stress, or personal distractions.

Here's how to overcome those barriers:

- Time Management – Schedule family time like you schedule meetings. Protect it.
- Energy Management – If work drains you, build transition time before engaging with your kids. A 10-minute walk or quiet moment can reset your mind.
- Prioritization – Ask yourself: If I don't show up for my kids now, who will? The job, the emails, and the to-do list will always be there. Your children's childhood won't.

YOUR PRESENCE IS YOUR LEGACY

When your children look back on their lives, they won't remember how many hours you worked or how much money you made.

They will remember how you made them feel.

They will remember the bedtime stories, the encouraging words, the way you looked at them with pride, and the times you stopped everything just to be with them.

Being a present father isn't just about today—it's about the lasting imprint you leave on your children's lives.

FINAL THOUGHT: SHOW UP. ENGAGE. LEAD.

Fatherhood is not about perfection—it's about consistency.

Your children need you. Not just your money, your job title, or your busy schedule.

They need you—fully present, fully engaged, and fully committed to leading them.

When you prioritize your presence, you're not just making a difference today—you're shaping the future of your children and the legacy you leave behind.

So, ask yourself: How will I show up today?

THE FATHERHOOD *by Design* GAME PLAN

Reflect:

How much time do I spend *fully present* with my kids each day?

What's one small change I can make today to be more intentional?

Commit: Spend 15–30 minutes of undistracted, one-on-one time with each child daily this week. Put away your phone. Let them lead. Be all-in.

At the end of the week, ask yourself:

Did I feel more connected?

Because the most powerful gift you can give your child isn't what you provide—it's how you show up.

YOUR PRESENCE IS THE POWER

You don't need all the answers. You don't have to be perfect. But your presence—your intentional, undistracted presence—is the greatest gift you can give your children.

Every moment you show up with purpose, you're shaping their identity, their confidence, and their future.

Ready to become more present and intentional as a father? Scan the QR code or visit www.erikwestrumbook.com to unlock your FREE 7-Day Fatherhood Challenge today.

Because the father they need... is you—fully present, fully engaged, fully alive.

CHAPTER 2

DISCIPLINE EQUALS FREEDOM IN PARENTING

"Discipline is choosing between what you want now and what you want most."

– Abraham Lincoln

When most people hear the word *discipline*, they think of punishment, rules, and restrictions. But in reality, discipline is not about control—it's about freedom.

When applied correctly, discipline creates an environment where children can thrive, develop confidence, and learn how to navigate life with responsibility and resilience.

As a father, I believe your role is not just to enforce rules, but to equip your children with the tools they need to succeed. Just like an athlete builds strength through structured training or a business leader thrives with daily discipline, parenting requires a clear framework of structure and consistency.

Without discipline, children grow up without direction, struggling to make decisions and face challenges. But when you instill discipline in your children's lives, you are teaching them how to create their own success, manage their emotions, and take ownership of their futures.

THE FIFTH KID

I had always thought of myself as a fun dad. The kind of dad who kept things light, joked around, made sure my kids had a good time. If there was a "cool parent" in our house, I wanted to be it.

But there was a problem.

My wife saw it before I did.

"You know you're the fifth kid in this family, right?" she said one night, arms crossed, watching me sink into the couch after a few too many drinks. The kids had been in bed for quite some time, but her words hit me like a slap to the face.

"What are you talking about?" I scoffed, though I already knew.

She sighed, shaking her head. "You expect the kids to be disciplined, but you're not. You tell them to show up, but you don't. You're asking them to be something you haven't figured out how to be yourself."

I wanted to argue. I wanted to tell her that I worked hard, that I provided, that I was there for them when it counted. But deep down, I knew she was right.

I wasn't leading—I was coasting.

I expected them to be disciplined with school, sports, and responsibilities, yet I lived on my own terms. Some nights, I'd have one drink too many, brushing off my sluggishness in the morning as "just a late night." I'd tell my kids to push themselves, to show up consistently, yet my own actions were inconsistent at best.

That conversation with my wife stuck with me. It was uncomfortable because it was true. I had been parenting from a place of expectation, not by example.

THE WAKE-UP CALL

The real shift came one morning when I stumbled out of bed late, rubbing the sleep from my eyes, my head pounding from the night before. I walked into the kitchen, expecting the usual morning chaos, but instead, I saw my wife sitting at the table, staring at her untouched breakfast.

"Why aren't you eating?" I asked, grabbing some coffee.

She shrugged. "Didn't feel like waking up early for church today? Do you even remember walking home?"

Her words were like a mirror.

That was me. That was exactly how I had been living. Making excuses. Saying I'd "be better next time." Expecting results without consistency.

I wanted to snap at her, to tell her discipline doesn't work that way, but I stopped myself. I had no authority in this conversation. I hadn't earned it.

It was in that moment that I saw, with painful clarity, that my wife and kids weren't just listening to what I said.

They were watching what I did.

And what they saw was a man who demanded discipline without living it.

THE TRANSFORMATION

That was the moment I decided enough was enough.

It started the next morning. No excuses. No "I'll start next week." I got up early. I read my Bible. I worked out. I committed to taking my personal growth seriously.

It wasn't easy at first. Waking up before the sun when my body wanted to stay in bed felt brutal. Choosing discipline over comfort was a daily battle. But I wasn't just doing it for me anymore.

I was doing it for *them*.

Weeks passed. Then months. My consistency became a routine. One morning, as I was finishing up a workout—drenched in sweat—my wife appeared in the doorway.

"You've been up early a lot," she said, rubbing her eyes.

"Yeah," I nodded. "Feels good."

She paused, then smiled. "Think I could work out with you sometime? Or maybe… just write me some workouts to start with?" She laughed, and we embraced. That was the moment I knew.

My transformation wasn't just about me getting better. It was about them *seeing* the standard I had set.

But it wasn't just my wife.

My kids began to notice too.

They saw the early mornings. They felt the shift in my presence, my patience, my purpose. Over time, they started asking to join me. Sometimes they'd wake up early just to sit nearby. Sometimes they'd mimic my stretches or ask questions about the Bible on the table. Little by little, my discipline was quietly becoming their blueprint.

I was no longer just asking my family to be disciplined.

I was *showing* them how.

Because true freedom doesn't come from doing whatever you want—it comes from knowing who you are and choosing what's best.

The more discipline you instill in your children today, the more freedom they'll have to succeed tomorrow.

DISCIPLINE IS A GIFT, NOT A PUNISHMENT

Many parents fall into two extremes when it comes to discipline:

Too Harsh – Authoritarian, rigid, controlling. This can lead to rebellion, fear, and resentment.

Too Lenient – Passive, avoiding conflict, letting kids "figure it out" on their own. This often creates entitlement, insecurity, and poor decision-making.

The best approach is firm but loving discipline—setting clear expectations, following through with consequences, and reinforcing lessons with patience and consistency.

Discipline should never be about anger—it should always be about growth.

Example:

If a child forgets to complete his or her chores, instead of yelling or letting it slide, a disciplined approach would be calmly reinforcing the expectation and implementing a fair consequence, such as losing screen time until the task is complete.

This teaches responsibility and accountability—not fear or avoidance.

WHY STRUCTURE CREATES FREEDOM

Some parents avoid discipline because they fear it will push their children away. But children actually thrive on structure.

Clear boundaries make them feel safe, secure, and confident in their environment.

When children know what is expected of them:

- They make better decisions because they understand cause and effect.
- They develop self-discipline, leading to success in school, sports, and personal goals.
- They feel loved and guided, knowing their father is invested in their growth.

Without discipline, children live in constant uncertainty:

- They don't know the rules, so they test boundaries.
- They don't understand the consequences, so they make reckless choices.
- They don't have structure, so they feel lost.

As a father, you must provide the structure that creates stability and the discipline that builds character.

DISCIPLINE IN ACTION: TEACHING KEY LIFE SKILLS

Discipline should be focused on teaching essential life skills that will serve your children in the long run.

Here's how discipline applies to key areas of growth:

Responsibility – Teach your children that choices have consequences. If they commit to something, they must follow through.

Respect – Model and enforce respect in words, actions, and attitudes toward parents, teachers, and others.

Work Ethic – Create a culture where effort, perseverance, and delayed gratification are celebrated.

Emotional Control – Teach children how to manage emotions without reacting impulsively. Help them pause, reflect, and respond with wisdom.

Time Management – Set routines and expectations that help children learn to balance work, play, and rest.

Integrity – Emphasize honesty, even when telling the truth is difficult.

LEADING BY EXAMPLE: YOUR DISCIPLINE SETS THE TONE

You cannot expect your children to develop discipline if you are not disciplined yourself.

If they see you procrastinating, making excuses, or avoiding responsibilities, they will do the same. But if they see you showing up with purpose and consistency, that becomes the model they internalize.

Fathers who lead with discipline in their own lives create a ripple effect in their families.

- If you wake up early and work hard, your children will learn the value of effort.
- If you follow through on commitments, your children will learn the importance of integrity.
- If you stay disciplined in your faith, fitness, and finances, your children will see what a strong foundation looks like.

But here's the thing: your children won't always *see* your discipline unless you let them in.

They may not fully understand your work ethic, your financial decisions, or the choices you make to protect your time and energy. That's why it's important to share the *why* behind your actions. Invite them into your world in age-appropriate ways. Tell them why you're getting up early. Let them know what you're saving for. Show them what faith looks like in practice—not just in words.

Children don't just hear what you say—they imitate what you *consistently* do.

Your example isn't just influencing their future—it's shaping their identity.

CREATING A FAMILY DISCIPLINE PLAN

To implement effective discipline in your home, it helps to have a Family Discipline Plan—a simple framework that outlines expectations, consequences, and core values.

Here's how to create one:

1. Define Core Family Values

Sit down as a family and discuss the key values that will guide your household (e.g., honesty, respect, hard work, kindness). This is similar to Exercise One you completed after Chapter One.

2. Set Clear Expectations

Outline what is expected from your children in different areas (school, chores, behavior, attitude). Make sure they understand the "why" behind the rules.

3. Establish Consequences

Consistent, fair consequences reinforce discipline. Make sure consequences fit the action (e.g., losing screen time for missing chores, extra responsibility for disrespect).

4. Model What You Expect

Make sure you are upholding the same standards you set for your children.

5. Have Family Check-Ins

Regularly discuss what's working and what needs improvement, and celebrate growth.

FINAL THOUGHT: DISCIPLINE IS LOVE

Discipline is not about control—it's about teaching.

When you discipline your children with love, consistency, and clear expectations, you give them the freedom to thrive.

If you do not teach them discipline, the world will—and often in much harsher ways.

The question is: Will you be the leader your children need to build a life of character, responsibility, and purpose?

Now is the time to step up, set the standard, and lead with discipline.

THE FATHERHOOD
by Design
GAME PLAN

Build Your Family Discipline Plan

1. **Choose 3 Core Values** you want to model and teach (e.g., Integrity, Hard Work, Respect).

2. **Define 3 Clear Expectations** for each value (e.g., Integrity = Tell the truth, keep your word, own your mistakes).

3. **Set Fair Consequences** when expectations aren't met (e.g., Disrespect = Apology + lost privileges).

4. **Be Consistent.** Enforce with love, not anger. Celebrate progress, not just perfection.

Strong discipline starts with clear values, fair structure, and steady leadership.

DISCIPLINE EQUALS FREEDOM—IN FATHERHOOD TOO

Structure. Consistency. Boundaries.
They're not just rules—they're the roadmap
to freedom for your family.

When you lead with discipline, you create stability.
When you model self-control, you empower your children.
And when your home has order, it becomes
a place of peace, growth, and purpose.

Ready to lead with intention and unlock true freedom in your parenting?
Scan the QR code or visit www.erikwestrumbook.com to begin your FREE 7-Day Fatherhood Challenge today.

Discipline isn't about control—it's about creating
the space for your family to thrive.

CHAPTER 3

LEADING BY EXAMPLE

"Your children will become who you are; so be who you want them to be."

– Unknown

Children are like mirrors—they reflect what they see in their parents. As a father, you are the first leader your children will follow, and whether you realize it or not, they are always watching.

They observe how you handle stress, how you treat their mother, how you manage responsibilities, and how you react to challenges. They absorb not just what you say, but what you do.

If you want your children to grow into disciplined, responsible, and purpose-driven individuals, you must first model those qualities yourself.

They will not do what you tell them to do—they will become a reflection of who you are.

YOUR DAILY HABITS SHAPE THEIR FUTURE

Think about your daily habits—not just the big moments, but the small, everyday choices you make. These are the lessons your children are absorbing:

- If they see you working hard, they will learn the value of effort.
- If they see you keeping your word, they will understand integrity.
- If they see you treating others with kindness and respect, they will do the same.
- If they see you making excuses, cutting corners, or avoiding responsibility, they will follow suit.

Your children will not become who you tell them to be—they will become a reflection of who you are.

THE POWER OF SMALL MOMENTS

Leadership is not just about the big lessons; it's about the small, everyday moments that shape a child's worldview.

- When you get up early to work out, your child sees discipline.
- When you apologize after making a mistake, your child learns humility.
- When you choose to pray before making a decision, your child learns faith.

- When you push through challenges instead of quitting, your child learns resilience.

These moments may seem small, but they add up to a lifetime of influence.

LEADING THROUGH HARD TIMES

Your children are watching how you respond to adversity.

Life will test you, and how you handle stress, disappointment, and failure will become the blueprint for how your children respond when life tests them.

- Do you get angry and lash out, or do you stay calm and problem-solve?
- Do you quit when things get hard, or do you push forward?
- Do you blame others, or do you take responsibility?

The way you handle challenges will shape how your children handle their own. They need to see strength, resilience, and emotional control modeled in you.

THE MOST IMPORTANT AREAS TO LEAD BY EXAMPLE

If you want to raise strong, disciplined children, you must lead by example in these key areas:

1. Work Ethic & Discipline

If you expect your children to work hard in school, sports, or their future careers, they need to see that same work ethic in you.

Example: Instead of just telling your child to finish their homework before playing video games, model discipline by finishing your own tasks first—whether it's work, a workout, or a home project.

2. Respect & Relationships

How you treat others—especially their mother—is the standard for how your children will treat people in their lives.

Example: Speak with kindness, show patience, and actively listen when they talk. Your interactions with them teach them how to communicate and respect others.

3. Faith & Moral Integrity

If faith is important to you, it should be evident in your actions, not just your words. Children need to see faith lived out, not just preached.

Example: Instead of just telling your kids to pray, invite them to pray with you. Read scripture together. Show them what a God-centered life looks like in action.

4. Health & Fitness

Taking care of your body isn't just about you—it's about setting an example of self-respect and discipline.

Example: Instead of just telling your kids to eat healthy and be active, involve them in workouts, outdoor activities, and meal prep so they learn firsthand.

5. Emotional Control & Character

Children need to see how to handle emotions like frustration, anger, and disappointment in a healthy way.

Example: When faced with a stressful situation, take a deep breath and calmly work through it. Show them that emotions are normal, but how we respond is a choice.

FATHERHOOD IN ALL ITS FORMS: NAVIGATING BLENDED AND EXTENDED FAMILIES

Not all families look the same—and neither does fatherhood.

Whether you're a stepdad, navigating a blended family, co-parenting across households, or raising children part-time due to shared custody, your role still matters deeply. And so do your challenges.

You may be working to earn trust with a child who didn't choose you. You may have to show restraint when dynamics get tense or when decisions are made outside of your control. Or maybe you're stepping into the role of father as a grandfather, uncle, or family friend. In any case—your presence still carries weight.

Here's the truth: intentional fatherhood isn't about having the perfect setup. It's about showing up, day in and day out, with love, consistency, and strength.

These principles—discipline, presence, communication, and legacy—apply in every fatherhood context. But in complex family dynamics, they may require more patience, more humility, and more grace. You may have to *earn* influence rather than assume it. And you may have to do it quietly, with a steady hand and an open heart.

Your role may not always come with a title or easy recognition.

But if you choose to lead with integrity, your impact will be just as real—and just as lasting.

Because every child deserves to see what love, leadership, and character look like in action, no matter what kind of family they come from.

YOUR LEGACY IS IN YOUR DAILY CHOICES

Your legacy isn't just about what you achieve—it's about who you are every day.

When your children look back, they won't remember every conversation, but they will remember how you lived.

What will they say about you?

- Will they remember a father who was disciplined, kind, and strong?
- Or will they remember a father who was distracted, reactive, and inconsistent?

The good news? You have the power to choose that legacy—starting today.

FINAL THOUGHT: BE THE MAN YOU WANT YOUR CHILDREN TO BECOME

Fatherhood is about showing, not just telling.

If you want to raise strong, disciplined, and purpose-driven children, you must first become that man yourself. But it doesn't stop there.

Your children need to *see* that man in action.

When they're young, they might not fully grasp what time you wake up, how you handle pressure at work, or the discipline behind your financial decisions. That's why as they grow, it's important to invite them into those unseen parts of your life. Share your routines. Talk about your challenges. Let them see what faith, perseverance, and purpose look like behind the scenes—not just in outcomes, but in effort.

Your children are always watching—but they can only learn from what you reveal.

What will they see?

More importantly—what will they *understand* because you chose to lead with both example *and* intentional engagement?

THE FATHERHOOD *by Design* GAME PLAN

Lead by Example: One Habit at a Time

Choose one habit you want your child to develop.

Be honest: Am I modeling this well?

Commit to improvement—write it down, make a simple plan, and take one small step today.

Great fathers don't just teach values—they live them. Start with one.

YOUR EXAMPLE IS THEIR BLUEPRINT

Your kids may hear what you say—but
they become what you *show.*

They're watching how you respond to pressure, how you treat others, how you love, lead, and live.
Every action is a lesson. Every moment is an opportunity.

You are the model they'll follow—
whether you mean to be or not.

Ready to lead with purpose and set a powerful example? Scan the QR code or visit www.erikwestrumbook.com to access your FREE 7-Day Fatherhood Challenge today.

Because real leadership doesn't demand—it demonstrates.
Start living the example they'll never forget.

CHAPTER 4

THE ROLE OF FAITH IN FATHERHOOD

"But as for me and my household,
we will serve the Lord."

– Joshua 24:15

Faith is the foundation of a strong, purpose-driven life. As a father, you are not just raising children—you are raising future leaders, men and women of integrity, and followers of Christ.

The values you instill today will shape how your children navigate life's challenges, make decisions, and develop their own relationship with God. Your role is not just to provide for them physically, but to equip them spiritually, giving them the strength to stand firm in an unpredictable world.

SCRUBS AND SILENCE: MY WAKE-UP CALL TO FAITH

I still remember that morning as if it were yesterday.

The air was crisp, the kind of early morning chill that seeps into your bones. But it wasn't the cold that sent shivers through me—it was the look in Kelly's eyes as I rolled out of the car at 7:10 a.m.

I had spent the night at a friend's house, and for whatever reason, I hadn't made it home. I didn't have a change of clothes, so I had thrown on a set of scrubs just to make it back. I still don't know if that made the situation better or worse.

I barely had time to register the judgment in Kelly's face before she snapped, "Get the kids to school."

No questions. No lecture. Just orders.

I turned around, feeling the daggers in her eyes piercing my back as I walked back to the car. The kids climbed in, confused but silent. And that's exactly how the drive went—dead silence.

I tried to justify it. I made excuse after excuse in my head, trying to prepare some half-decent explanation for why I hadn't come home, why I was wearing scrubs when I wasn't a doctor, why this wasn't as bad as it seemed. But I knew the truth.

I had been living with one foot in and one foot out.

A SUNDAY-ONLY CHRISTIAN

I had spent years talking about faith. Telling my kids about Jesus. Wanting them to have a relationship with Him. But what kind of example was I setting?

I was a Sunday-Only Christian.

I showed up to church, nodded at the right moments, maybe even felt something during worship. But Monday through Saturday? I lived however I wanted. I was halfway in, halfway out, treating my faith like a membership card I could flash when it was convenient and tuck away when it wasn't.

That car ride was the longest, most uncomfortable silence I had ever experienced. And for the first time, I really felt the weight of my own hypocrisy.

THE BREAKING POINT

That night, I sat alone in the living room. No distractions. No noise. Just me and the truth I had been avoiding.

I had spent so much time trying to lead my family, yet I was the one who was lost. I was telling my kids to follow Jesus while I was barely following Him myself. I was trying to instill values I wasn't even living out.

And that's when it hit me.

I couldn't fake this. I couldn't be halfway in. I couldn't expect my kids to take their faith seriously if I wasn't willing to take mine seriously.

I didn't need a fresh start. I needed to surrender.

So that night, I dropped to my knees and prayed—really prayed. Not the quick, routine prayers I had muttered for years, but a desperate, broken, I-can't-do-this-alone kind of prayer.

I asked God to change me from the inside out. To take my half-hearted faith and make it whole. To show me how to truly lead my family—not just by what I said, but by how I lived.

And that's where the transformation began.

ALL IN

It wasn't overnight. But little by little, things changed.

I woke up early—not just to go through the motions, but to spend real time in the Word. I didn't just talk about Jesus—I walked with Him. My kids started seeing a different version of me—not the guy who preached one thing and lived another, but a father who was fully committed to the faith he wanted them to follow.

I was done being a Sunday-Only Christian.

I was all in.

And the most powerful part? My family noticed. My kids saw the shift. My wife saw the consistency. The respect I had lost that morning in scrubs, I was slowly earning back—not because of words, but because of action.

That drive of shame in silence became a turning point.

And I'll never forget the lesson:

Faith isn't about what you say—it's about how you live.

Faith is the anchor in life's storms. Life will bring hardships, failures, and moments of doubt. What will your children turn to in those moments?

A father who leads his home in faith provides his children with a firm foundation—one that teaches them:

- God is always present, even in struggles.
- Their identity is found in Christ, not in the world.
- True success is measured by faith, character, and obedience to God's will.
- No matter how far they stray, they can always return to Him.

When your children see you turning to God in your own struggles, they learn that faith is not just a belief—it's a way of life.

YOUR RESPONSIBILITY AS A SPIRITUAL LEADER

Many fathers assume that teaching faith is the job of the church, a Christian school, or their children's mother. But God has called fathers to be the spiritual leaders of their homes.

Ephesians 6:4 reminds us:

"Fathers, do not provoke your children to anger, but bring them up in the discipline and instruction of the Lord."

This means you must be intentional about:

- Teaching your children biblical truths

- Modeling faith through your actions
- Making God the center of your home

If faith is going to be a strong foundation in your home, it needs to be more than something you do on Sundays. It should be woven into your daily life.

HOW TO LEAD YOUR FAMILY IN FAITH

I don't seek to be the blessing—just a blessing in someone's journey.

Here are five practical ways to lead your family in faith:

1. Pray with Your Children

Prayer should be more than a habit; it should be a lifeline. Let your children see you praying not just in crisis, but in gratitude, in decision-making, and in daily life.

Example: Start a tradition of praying before meals, bedtime, or before big decisions. Teach your children that they can talk to God anytime.

2. Read Scripture Together

The Bible is the ultimate guide for life. Your children need to hear and see you engaging with God's Word.

Example: Set aside time each week for a family devotional. Read a passage, discuss its meaning, and pray together. Let your children ask questions and be part of the conversation.

3. Live Out Your Faith

Your children will learn more from what you do than what you say. If you want them to have a strong faith, they need to see it actively lived out in your life.

Example: Model godly character in how you treat others, handle stress, and make decisions. Show them what it looks like to walk in faith even when life is hard.

4. Serve Others Together

Faith isn't just about belief—it's about action. Jesus calls us to love and serve others, and your children should see you doing this in real ways.

Example: Volunteer as a family, support those in need, or practice generosity and kindness in your community.

5. Create a Culture of Gratitude & Worship

A home built on faith should be filled with gratitude, worship, and joy in the Lord. Teach your children to recognize and thank God for His blessings.

Example: Start a "gratitude journal" where each family member writes one thing they're thankful for each day. Play worship music in your home and encourage your kids to sing along.

FAITH & RESILIENCE: HELPING YOUR KIDS STAND FIRM

Leading your family is not always easy, and that is why one of the most powerful gifts faith provides is resilience.

The world will try to tell your children who they should be. It will throw obstacles in their way, tempt them with distractions, and challenge their beliefs. But a child grounded in faith is unshakable.

- They will know their worth comes from God, not from social media or the opinions of others.
- They will turn to prayer instead of fear when faced with uncertainty.
- They will have the strength to make choices based on faith, not pressure.

When fathers model a strong, unwavering faith, children grow up knowing that no matter what happens, God is with them.

FINAL THOUGHT: BUILDING A LEGACY OF FAITH

At the end of your life, the greatest thing you can pass down to your children is not money, success, or status—it's faith.

When your children face difficulties, they will remember the prayers you prayed over them.

When they struggle with doubt, they will recall the way you trusted God.

When they have families of their own, they will carry forward the faith you instilled in them.

Fatherhood is temporary, but the spiritual legacy you leave will last for generations.

What kind of legacy will you leave?

The Fatherhood *by Design* Game Plan

Start a Weekly Devotional or Prayer Time

Faith doesn't grow by accident—it grows by intention.

This week, commit to leading your family in a simple, meaningful devotional or prayer time. Here's how to begin:

Pick a Day & Time

Choose a consistent time that works for your family (e.g., Sunday night or Saturday morning).

Choose a Scripture

Select a short Bible passage to read together and reflect on.

Ask a Question

Engage your children by asking: *"What does this mean to you?"* or *"How can we apply this today?"*

Pray Together

Have each family member share a prayer request, then pray as a family.

Stay Consistent

Don't aim for perfection—aim for presence. The habit of showing up matters more than getting it all right.

Because when you lead your family spiritually,
you're planting seeds that will grow for generations.

FAITH IS YOUR FOUNDATION

Fatherhood isn't just a role—it's a calling.
And to lead your family well, you need more than strength…
You need faith.

Faith grounds you when life gets chaotic.
It gives you wisdom when you feel unsure.
And it reminds you that you're never leading alone.

Want to grow as a faith-filled father?
Scan the QR code or visit www.erikwestrumbook.com to access your FREE 7-Day Fatherhood Challenge today.

Because a father rooted in faith becomes a source of strength for generations.
Lead with faith. Lead by design.

CHAPTER 5

RAISING MENTALLY TOUGH KIDS

"Hard times create strong men. Strong men create good times. Good times create weak men. Weak men create hard times."

— Michael Hopf

Life is not easy, and it never will be. Your children will face disappointment, failure, rejection, and hardship. Your job as a father is not to shield them from challenges, but to equip them to handle them with strength, resilience, and confidence.

In a world that often promotes comfort and ease, mentally tough kids stand out. They know how to push through difficulty, solve problems, take responsibility, and stay committed to their goals. Mental toughness is the key to success in all areas of life—school, sports, relationships, faith, and career.

THE LESSON THAT CHANGED EVERYTHING

Eighth grade was supposed to be my year. I had worked hard, played my heart out, and felt like I had a real shot at making the A hockey team. I could already picture it—wearing that jersey, playing with the best, proving to everyone that I belonged at the top of my team.

But then, reality hit like a punch to the gut.

I got the phone call.

I had been cut.

I stood there, my heart pounding, my stomach twisting into knots. This had to be a mistake. I had outplayed some of the kids who made it. I had put in the effort. I deserved it.

Or at least, that's what I told myself.

Anger burned in my chest. I blamed the evaluators and the coaches—maybe they had favorites. I blamed the other players—maybe they got lucky. I blamed everything and everyone except the one person who mattered: me.

THE TALK WITH MY DAD

I threw the phone down and sat on my couch at home, still fuming. My dad was waiting for me, sitting in his usual spot in the living room. He could tell something was wrong the second I threw down the phone.

"What happened?" he asked.

I barely got the words out. "I got cut."

I expected sympathy. Maybe even a little outrage on my behalf. But instead, he nodded, as if he had already expected it.

And then he said something I'll never forget.

"Maybe you deserved it. Maybe you didn't. But the reality is, you have two choices. You can blame others, or you can put in the work when no one else is looking."

I stared at him, waiting for more. Waiting for him to say how unfair it was, how I should've made it, how the coaches had made a mistake.

But he didn't.

Instead, he leaned forward and looked me dead in the eye. "What are you going to do about it?"

THE LONG ROAD TO MENTAL TOUGHNESS

I wish I could say I took his advice that night, that I immediately flipped a switch and started training harder than ever. But I didn't.

For weeks, I sulked. I avoided talking about it. I let the bitterness eat away at me. And every time I wanted to complain, my dad's words echoed in my mind.

What are you going to do about it?

Eventually, the sting of rejection faded just enough for me to see things clearly. If I wanted to make the team next year, if I wanted to prove I belonged, I had to stop feeling sorry for myself and outwork everyone else.

So, I did.

I shot pucks every day. I stayed after practice, working on my game, my speed, my endurance. I lifted weights. I studied the game. I pushed myself harder than I ever had before—not because anyone was watching, but because I refused to let that failure define me.

By the time the next tryouts came around, I wasn't the same player. I had transformed—not just physically, but mentally. I skated onto the ice knowing that no one had outworked me. I had already won before the first drill even started.

This time, my name was on the roster.

THE LESSON THAT LASTED A LIFETIME

Looking back, getting cut from that team was the best thing that ever happened to me. Because it forced me to take ownership of my life.

That lesson—that I could decide my own outcome by how I showed up—stuck with me long after hockey. It shaped how I approached every obstacle, every challenge, every failure. It made me mentally tough.

And now, as a father, I tell my kids that same story. Not to scare them. Not to make them feel like failure is the enemy. But to show them that setbacks are opportunities. That every challenge is a test of character.

That when life knocks you down, you have two choices:

Blame others.

Or put in the work when no one else is looking.

I know which one I chose. And I know which one I want them to choose, too.

The good news? Mental toughness isn't something a child is born with—it's something that's developed. And as their father, you play the biggest role in shaping it.

WHAT IS MENTAL TOUGHNESS?

Mental toughness isn't about being cold, emotionless, or never struggling. Instead, it's about developing the mindset and skills needed to face challenges without breaking down, giving up, or making excuses.

A mentally tough child has:

- Perseverance – They keep going even when things get hard.
- Emotional Control – They don't let frustration or fear control their decisions.
- Problem-Solving Skills – They focus on solutions instead of complaining about problems.
- Discipline – They follow through on commitments even when they don't feel like it.
- Resilience – They bounce back from failure instead of quitting.

These are skills that will serve them for life—in school, sports, relationships, and eventually, their careers.

WHY KIDS NEED TO EXPERIENCE HARD THINGS

Many parents unintentionally weaken their children by making life too easy for them. They step in too quickly when their kids struggle, removing obstacles instead of teaching them how to overcome them.

- A child who never has to work hard won't develop perseverance.
- A child who is never allowed to fail won't learn how to bounce back.
- A child who is always rescued won't learn how to solve problems.

Mental toughness is built through experience, not words. Your kids need to struggle. They need to face challenges. They need to learn through action, not just advice.

As their father, your role is not to remove hardship—it's to walk alongside them as they push through it.

TEACHING MENTAL TOUGHNESS THROUGH EVERYDAY LIFE

You don't need extreme experiences to build mental toughness in your kids. Everyday life provides opportunities to teach perseverance, discipline, and resilience.

Here are practical ways to help your children develop mental toughness:

1. Encourage Problem-Solving Instead of Rescue

When your child faces a challenge, don't jump in and solve it for them. Instead, guide them through problem-solving.

Example: If they forget their homework at school, resist the urge to rush back and get it. Instead, ask: "What's your plan to fix this?" This teaches responsibility and critical thinking.

2. Let Them Experience Failure

Failure is one of the best teachers in life—if we let it be. Teach your kids that failure is not the end—it's a step toward growth.

Example: If they lose a game or get a bad grade, instead of saying, "It's okay, it doesn't matter," ask: "What did you learn? How will you improve next time?" This shifts their mindset from failure being shameful to failure being a lesson.

3. Push Through Discomfort

Teach your children to do things even when they don't feel like it. Mental toughness is built in the moments when they want to quit but choose to keep going.

Example: If they start a sport or activity, don't let them quit the moment it gets hard. Teach them to finish what they start, even if it's uncomfortable.

4. Teach Emotional Control

Life will bring frustration, disappointment, and fear. Mentally tough kids know how to handle emotions without letting them dictate their actions.

Example: If your child gets frustrated when learning something new, teach them how to take a deep breath, reset, and keep trying. Respond with calm, not frustration.

5. Develop Physical Toughness to Build Mental Toughness

There is a direct connection between physical challenges and mental resilience. Hard physical activity teaches kids discipline, perseverance, and how to push through discomfort.

Example: Encourage your kids to engage in physical challenges—sports, workouts, hiking, or even cold showers. Teach them that their bodies and minds are capable of more than they think.

RAISING A "NO-EXCUSES" MINDSET

One of the biggest killers of mental toughness is excuses. The moment kids learn to justify quitting, blaming others, or avoiding hard things, they weaken their resilience.

As a father, set a no-excuses standard in your home.

- If they make a mistake, they should own it instead of blaming others.
- If they commit to something, they need to follow through even when it gets hard.

- If they don't feel like doing something, remind them that discipline is more important than feelings.

The goal is not to be harsh—it's to raise kids who don't crumble under pressure.

FINAL THOUGHT: YOUR KIDS WILL BE AS STRONG AS YOU TEACH THEM TO BE

Mentally tough kids don't just happen—they are trained. They are built through intentional challenges, resilience-building experiences, and a father who leads by example.

The world is tough. Prepare your children to be tougher.

What kind of resilience will your kids develop because of the lessons you teach them today?

THE FATHERHOOD *by Design* GAME PLAN

Build a Challenge List

Mental toughness grows outside the comfort zone. This week, sit down with your child and create a **Challenge List**—simple, age-appropriate tasks that push them to grow.

Explain why challenges help us grow.

Brainstorm 5–10 challenges based on their age and interests.

Young kids: memorize a Bible verse, try a new food, run a mile.

Teens: speak in public, fast from tech, do a tough workout.

Pick one challenge to complete this week.

Celebrate effort over perfection—growth is the goal.

Because confidence is built in challenge—and you get to lead them through it.

RAISING MENTALLY TOUGH KIDS STARTS WITH YOU

Your children won't develop grit, resilience, or confidence by accident.
They learn it by watching how you lead through challenge.
Mental toughness starts at home—with fathers who model strength, courage, and consistency.

Let your kids see what it looks like to push through, not give up.
To stay grounded when life gets hard.
To rise after failure—and keep going.

Want to raise mentally strong, confident kids?
Scan the QR code or visit www.erikwestrumbook.com to access your FREE 7-Day Fatherhood Challenge today.

Because tough times will come—prepare your kids to rise, not retreat.
It starts with how *you* lead.

CHAPTER 6

THE IMPORTANCE OF COMMUNICATION & CONNECTION

"The way we talk to our children becomes their inner voice."

– Peggy O'Mara

Fatherhood is more than just providing for your children—it's about building a strong relationship with them. And at the core of any strong relationship is communication and connection.

Your words and actions shape your child's confidence, emotional intelligence, and ability to form relationships. But communication is more than just talking—it's about building a foundation of trust. The way you engage with your children today will determine whether they feel comfortable coming to you with their struggles, questions, and dreams in the future.

DISCONNECTED IN A CONNECTED WORLD

The years of COVID weren't just a crisis for the world—they were a crisis for our family.

At first, it seemed like we were all together, spending more time in the same space than ever before. But in reality, we were miles apart. Physically in the same house, but mentally and emotionally distant.

Every day was the same cycle. The kids had school, but instead of real classrooms and real connections, there were screens—computer screens, iPads, endless Zoom meetings. My work wasn't much different. Call after call, meeting after meeting, I was present in body but absent in mind. And when the day finally came to an end, there were more screens. Movies, TV shows, anything to distract from the stress and uncertainty.

Somewhere along the way, our conversations became transactional. "Did you finish your schoolwork?" "What do you want for dinner?" "Time for bed." We were speaking, but we weren't talking. We were coexisting, but we weren't connecting.

And in the middle of it all, we had a newborn and three other kids under the age of 12. It was a juggling act just to keep things moving, to survive another day. And survival mode became the norm.

The worst part? I didn't even realize how far we had drifted.

FILLING THE WRONG BUCKETS

If that wasn't enough, I was also coaching high school hockey.

For eight years, I poured into other kids' lives—mentoring, motivating, pushing them to be better, teaching them lessons about hard work, accountability, and discipline. I was all in.

And I loved it.

It filled my bucket. Watching those kids grow, seeing them succeed, knowing I had an impact—it gave me a purpose outside of work, outside of the chaos of life. Coaching was my escape.

But while I was filling my bucket, I wasn't filling my children's buckets.

I was more worried about our team's roster than my own kids' report cards. More invested in pre-game speeches than bedtime stories. More focused on shaping teenage athletes than shaping the hearts of my own children.

And then it hit me.

I was giving the best of me to kids who would eventually move on, graduate, and go their own way—while my own kids were at home, getting whatever was left over.

I was disconnected.

THE HARDEST DECISION, THE RIGHT DECISION

The realization came slowly, and then all at once.

One night, after another long day of screens, noise, and exhaustion, I walked into the living room and saw my kids sitting on the couch—each one glued to a device. Not talking. Not playing. Just there.

It was like looking in a mirror.

I thought about all the hours I spent coaching other kids, while my own were growing up without me fully present. I thought about how I expected them to talk to me, but I wasn't creating space to listen. I thought about how I was so focused on making an impact in the world yet missing the biggest impact I was called to make—in my own home.

That's when it changed.

I made the decision to step away from coaching. It wasn't easy—I had poured years into it. But I knew if I didn't make a shift, I'd look back with regret. My kids didn't need a coach.

They needed their dad.

CHOOSING CONNECTION OVER CONVENIENCE

At first, it was awkward.

Without hockey, without the constant grind, I had to relearn how to be present. How to have real conversations with my kids instead of just checking in. How to sit with them, listen, ask questions, and actually hear their answers.

We set limits on screen time—not just for them, but for me too. We played games, had real meals together, and started talking again. I didn't just ask about their grades—I asked about their struggles, their dreams, their worries.

And the more I leaned in, the more I realized something painful:

They had been waiting for me.

Waiting for me to notice.

Waiting for me to be all in on them the way I had been for everyone else.

NO MORE HALF-IN, HALF-OUT

Stepping away from coaching didn't mean I stopped mentoring. It didn't mean I stopped making an impact. It meant I finally put first things first.

It meant I no longer gave the best of me to the outside world and the rest of me to my family.

I wasn't perfect. I never will be. But for the first time in a long time, I was fully present.

And that—more than anything else—was the greatest impact I could ever make.

As a father, you set the tone for open, honest, and meaningful conversations. Your ability to communicate with your children directly affects:

- Their self-esteem – Children who feel heard develop confidence in expressing their thoughts.

- Their emotional intelligence – Kids who learn to communicate well can better handle emotions and relationships.
- Their trust in you – If they know they can talk to you about small things, they'll come to you with big things.
- Their ability to problem-solve – Open communication teaches them how to navigate challenges with clarity.

Fathers who actively communicate and connect with their children create an unshakable foundation of love, trust, and security.

BARRIERS TO EFFECTIVE COMMUNICATION

Many fathers struggle with communication, not because they don't care, but because they were never taught how to engage emotionally. Here are some common barriers:

- Distractions – Phones, work, and stress can make it easy to be physically present but mentally absent.
- Lack of Emotional Availability – Some men struggle to express feelings or listen to emotions without immediately trying to "fix" the problem.
- One-Way Conversations – Talking at your child instead of talking with them.
- Avoiding Difficult Topics – Some fathers shy away from deep discussions, assuming their kids will figure things out on their own.

But communication is a skill—and like any skill, it can be learned and strengthened with practice.

MASTERING CONFLICT WITH GRACE

Conflict is inevitable in any household, but how we handle disagreements teaches our children valuable lessons about communication, emotional control, and problem-solving.

Children are watching how you handle stress, arguments, and disappointments. If they see you:

- Resolving conflicts calmly and with respect, they will learn to do the same.
- Reacting with anger and blame, they will mirror that behavior.

How you handle conflict today will shape how your children navigate relationships, work, and life challenges in the future.

DEVELOPING SKILLS FOR EFFECTIVE CONFLICT RESOLUTION

Handling conflict is like steering a ship through stormy seas. Your goal is to reach calm waters without damaging relationships.

Here's how you can model effective conflict resolution:

- Stay Calm & Listen – Anger escalates problems. Show your children that real strength is in staying composed and listening first.
- Use "I" Statements – Instead of saying, "You always make a mess!" try "I feel frustrated when the house

is cluttered." This shifts the focus from blame to problem-solving.

- Encourage Solutions – In disagreements, ask rhetorical questions like, "How can we fix this together?" to get your child thinking about problem-solving instead of arguing.

- Model Apologizing & Forgiveness – If you react poorly, own it, and apologize. This teaches your children that real leadership includes humility.

HOW TO BUILD STRONGER COMMUNICATION WITH YOUR CHILDREN

The good news is that you don't have to be a perfect communicator to connect with your child—you just need to be intentional. Here's how:

1. Be Present & Attentive

Your child knows when you're fully engaged versus when you're distracted. Set aside intentional time to connect.

- Example: Put your phone away and make eye contact when your child talks to you.

- Example: Set a tradition where you and each child have one-on-one time each week.

2. Listen More Than You Speak

Most fathers want to teach, correct, or give advice—but sometimes, your child just needs to be heard.

- Example: Instead of jumping in with solutions, try saying, "That sounds really tough. Tell me more about how you're feeling."

- Example: When your child shares something, reflect it back: "I hear you saying that you're frustrated because your friend ignored you today. That must have been hard."

Listening builds trust. When your child feels heard, they will be more likely to open up in the future.

3. Use the "Ask, Listen, Share" Method

To encourage meaningful conversations, use this simple three-step framework:

- Ask: Start with an open-ended question. "What was the best part of your day?" or "What's something you're excited about right now?"

- Listen: Give them space to respond without interrupting. Show interest and ask follow-up questions.

- Share: Respond in a way that connects—share a similar experience or affirm their emotions before giving advice.

4. Create a Safe Space for Honest Conversations

Your child should feel safe expressing their thoughts, emotions, and mistakes without fear of judgment.

- Example: If your child messes up, don't react with anger first. Instead, say, "Let's talk about what happened. I want to understand your perspective."
- Example: If they express a struggle, instead of dismissing it, acknowledge their feelings: "That sounds really tough. How can I help?"

The safer your child feels with you, the more they will come to you when it matters most.

BONDING THROUGH SHARED ACTIVITIES

Communication isn't just about words—it's about shared experiences. The time you spend engaging in activities together is just as important as the conversations you have.

When you engage in your child's world, you:

- Strengthen your bond.
- Build a relationship of trust where they feel safe opening up.
- Create opportunities for organic, natural conversations.

HOW TO CONNECT THROUGH SHARED ACTIVITIES

Find Common Ground

Pick activities you both enjoy. Whether it's sports, board games, reading, or hiking, find something that creates shared joy.

Be Fully Present

Put away distractions—no phones, no emails, no multitasking. Give your child your full attention.

Teach Through Action

Whether it's fishing, woodworking, or playing a game, use the activity to teach life lessons about perseverance, teamwork, and problem-solving.

Example: A father who teaches his child how to fish is not just teaching fishing—he's teaching patience, focus, and the reward of persistence.

BUILDING LASTING TRADITIONS

Consistency is key. Make shared activities a regular habit—not just a one-time event.

- Car Ride Conversations – Instead of playing music, use the drive to ask questions.
- Dinner Table Talks – Make meals a time for open discussion.
- Bedtime Check-Ins – Ask your child, "What's one thing that made you happy today?" before they sleep.
- "No-Phone" Walks – Go for a walk together without distractions.

These simple moments may seem small, but over time, they build a deep and lasting connection.

FINAL THOUGHT: YOUR WORDS SHAPE THEIR WORLD

The way you communicate and connect with your children today will shape their confidence, emotional intelligence, and willingness to open up in the future.

Fathers who are intentional about communication and connection create a home where their children feel valued, understood, and safe to express themselves.

The best time to build this connection is now.

Your child is watching. How will you show up today?

THE FATHERHOOD *by Design* GAME PLAN

Connect Through Conversation & Bonding

1. Have a Heart-to-Heart

Choose a relaxed time and use the **Ask, Listen, Share** method:

- **Ask** a thoughtful question
- **Listen** without interrupting
- **Share** your experience or encouragement

Keep it safe and judgment-free—the goal is connection, not correction.

2. Plan a One-on-One Activity

Let your child choose something they love. Be fully present.

If it goes well, make it a weekly or monthly tradition.

Because real connection happens when your presence says, "You matter to me."

CONNECTION BEGINS WITH COMMUNICATION

Your kids don't need more perfection—they need more *connection.*
And connection starts with conversation.

When you take the time to listen, ask questions, and be fully present, you're building trust, shaping identity, and showing your child they matter.

Strong fathers don't just speak—they *connect.*

Ready to strengthen the bond with your children?
Scan the QR code or visit www.erikwestrumbook.com to access your FREE 7-Day Fatherhood Challenge today.

Because the words you say—and the ones you truly hear—can change everything.
Lead with love. Communicate with purpose. Connect by design.

CHAPTER 7

DISCIPLINE IN DAILY HABITS: BALANCING FATHERHOOD AND WORK-LIFE HARMONY

"We are what we repeatedly do. Excellence, then, is not an act, but a habit."

– Aristotle

Fatherhood is not defined by a single grand moment—it is shaped in the small, consistent actions of daily life. The habits you cultivate, the time you dedicate, and the structure you provide will determine the character, resilience, and future success of your children.

As a father, you are the standard-bearer of discipline, connection, and leadership in your home. Your children will follow your example—whether good or bad. If you model consistency, integrity, and purpose, they will learn to do the same.

THE HUSTLE AND THE HOME

Retiring from professional hockey wasn't the hard part.

The hard part was what came next.

For years, my life had been structured around the game. Training, travel, competition—I had a purpose every single day. And then, suddenly, it was over. The ice, the locker room, the adrenaline—all of it was gone.

But I wasn't the type to sit still. I knew I had to channel my energy into something new, and that something was starting my own business.

I was all in.

Late nights. Early mornings. Coffee-fueled meetings. The constant hustle of building something from nothing. And when I wasn't working? I was "networking"—which, if I'm being honest, was just another excuse to keep working.

The lines blurred quickly.

I told myself I was doing it for my family, that every deal I closed, every connection I made, was to create a better future for them. But deep down, I knew the truth:

I was addicted to the grind.

THE COST OF SUCCESS

The problem with success is that it doesn't come with a warning label. No one tells you that chasing your dreams can make you blind to what really matters.

I justified the late nights because "just one more meeting" could mean a new deal. I rationalized missing dinners because "this client could change everything." I convinced myself that my presence at home could wait, because work had to come first—at least for now.

But "for now" turned into weeks.

Then months.

And one night, I came home late—again. The house was dark except for the soft glow of the kitchen light. My wife, Kelly, was sitting at the table, a cold plate of food pushed to the side.

She didn't yell. She didn't need to.

"You're never home for dinner," she said quietly, her voice carrying more weight than if she had shouted.

I started to defend myself, to explain how I was doing this for us, for the future. But before I could speak, she said something that stopped me cold:

"By the time you finally slow down, will we even be here waiting?"

That hit me like a puck to the face.

THE BALANCE SHIFT

That night, I sat alone in my office, staring at my calendar. Every hour of my day was scheduled—meetings, calls, and networking events. Nowhere on that schedule was time for my family.

I had convinced myself that working hard was the only way to provide for them. But providing wasn't just about money. It was about being there.

Being present.

That's when I made a decision.

I wasn't going to work less hard—because hard work was part of who I was. But I was going to work smarter.

I set clear work hours. When I was working, I was all in. But when I wasn't? I was home—fully home. No phones at the dinner table. No checking emails during family time. No half-listening to my kids while my mind was on my next deal.

I scheduled time with my family the same way I scheduled meetings—because if it wasn't on the calendar, I knew it wouldn't happen.

THE POWER OF PRESENCE

It didn't take long to see the difference.

My kids lit up when I actually showed up—not just physically, but mentally and emotionally. I wasn't just a provider. I was their dad.

And the crazy thing? My business didn't suffer. In fact, it thrived.

Why? Because when I was working, I was locked in. No distractions. No wasted time. Just focused, intentional effort. And when I wasn't working? I was present, recharged, and ready to give my best to the people who mattered most.

That's the balance so many people miss.

Success isn't about working non-stop. It's about knowing when to go all in—and when to step away.

Because at the end of the day, business deals will come and go. But family? That's the real legacy.

And I wasn't about to lose mine.

That's why this chapter is about taking ownership of your role as a father by designing a disciplined, meaningful routine that fosters growth, connection, and leadership while also balancing the demands of work and family life. Yes, we are digging deeper into discipline again. The importance of embracing discipline is so vital to the impact you will make today, tomorrow, and into the future as a father pouring into your kids.

THE POWER OF DAILY HABITS IN FATHERHOOD

Children thrive in structured, predictable environments. They feel safe, confident, and empowered when they know what to expect. The routines you establish teach them discipline, responsibility, and the power of consistency.

- Morning habits set the tone for the day.
- Bedtime routines provide security and connection
- Family rituals build trust and strengthen relationships.
- Daily disciplines teach self-control and accountability.

Every day is an opportunity to shape your children's mindset, values, and work ethic through intentional habits.

YOUR CHILDREN ARE WATCHING—LEAD BY EXAMPLE

As a father, remember that your actions will influence your children far more than your words do.

- If you wake up early and start your day with purpose, they will learn the value of discipline.
- If you prioritize family time over distractions, they will understand the importance of connection.
- If you follow through on responsibilities, they will learn integrity.

Your daily habits create the culture of your home. Are they leading your children toward success, stability, and character—or reinforcing inconsistency and chaos?

Your children are watching. What are your habits teaching them?

CREATING A DISCIPLINED FAMILY CULTURE

Again, the goal is to build a structured but flexible home environment where discipline is part of daily life. Here's where it matters most:

1. The Power of a Strong Morning Routine

A strong morning routine builds momentum, focus, and discipline.

- Wake up early – Show your children that success starts with intentionality.
- Faith or gratitude practice – Start the day with prayer or a positive mindset.
- Physical activity – Exercise creates energy and focus.
- Family check-in – A quick breakfast or chat fosters connection.

Example: Instead of rushing out the door, set a structured routine where your kids wake up consistently, make their beds, and have a healthy start to the day.

2. Establishing Meaningful Connection Points

Family meals and rituals are some of the most powerful habits you can build. Studies show families who eat together:

- Have stronger relationships
- Develop better communication skills
- Raise healthier, more confident children

Example: Make dinner a non-negotiable family time, even if it's just 15-30 minutes together without distractions.

3. Teaching Discipline Through Responsibilities

Children must learn that success requires effort, consistency, and personal responsibility.

- Time management – Completing tasks on time
- Accountability – Following through on commitments

- Teamwork – Contributing to the family unit

Example: Create a chore system where kids earn privileges based on responsibility, reinforcing the habit of earning rewards through effort.

4. Evening & Bedtime Routines for Stability

A structured evening routine signals the brain to slow down, promotes better sleep, and reinforces discipline.

- Wind down intentionally – Limit screen time before bed.
- Reflect on the day – Encourage gratitude and positive thinking.
- Read, pray, or share a story – End the night with connection.

Example: Instead of kids falling asleep with screens, create a bedtime ritual where you read together, pray, and reflect on the day's lessons.

BALANCING WORK & FATHERHOOD–MASTERING THE JUGGLE

In today's fast-paced world, fathers often struggle to balance demanding careers with active parenting. The pressure to excel at work while being present at home can lead to stress and guilt. But mastering this balance is not only possible—it's essential for both your personal fulfillment and your family's well-being.

Here's how:

1. Prioritize & Schedule Dedicated Family Time

Time is your most valuable asset. You cannot get back missed moments with your children. Set family time as a non-negotiable priority.

- Use a digital calendar – Schedule family activities like you do work meetings.
- Create a family tradition – Weekly game night, Sunday breakfast, or outdoor adventures.
- Be fully present – No distractions, just quality time together.

Example: Treat family dinner like a boardroom meeting—schedule it, commit to it, and show up on time.

2. Work Smarter, Not Harder

You don't need more hours—you need better time management.

- Plan your workweek – Prioritize the most important tasks first.
- Set clear boundaries – No emails or work calls during family time.
- Maximize efficiency – Focus on high-impact work instead of being busy.

Example: Cut unnecessary meetings and delegate minor tasks to free up time for your family.

3. Reduce Parenting Stress by Setting Realistic Goals

Being a great father doesn't require perfection—it requires presence.

- Set achievable expectations – Stop trying to "do it all" and focus on what matters most.
- Involve your children in daily tasks – Cooking, cleaning, and errands can be bonding moments.
- Ask for help – Lean on your spouse, family, or friends for support.

Example: Instead of feeling guilty for missing a school event, schedule quality one-on-one time to connect.

FINAL THOUGHT: YOUR DAILY DISCIPLINE DETERMINES YOUR LEGACY

A father's greatest impact isn't made in one big moment—it's made in the small, daily disciplines that shape his children's lives.

The time you spend with your children today will shape who they become tomorrow.

What kind of daily discipline will define your fatherhood?

The choice is yours.

THE FATHERHOOD *by Design* GAME PLAN

Build Your Fatherhood Blueprint

Create a simple framework to lead your family with **discipline, connection, and balance**:

Define Your Priorities

What values should your daily habits reflect? (e.g., Faith, Discipline, Connection)

Create Non-Negotiable Routines

- Morning structure
- Family connection time
- Chores & responsibilities
- Evening wind-down

Master Time Management

Schedule family time, set boundaries, and work with focus.

Stay Consistent—but Adaptable

Be steady, but flexible when life shifts. Never compromise your core values.

Start tomorrow. Write your plan:

- Morning Routine:
- Daily Connection Time:
- Chores/Responsibilities:
- Evening Ritual:
- My Personal Discipline Focus:

Because the structure you build today becomes the foundation they stand on tomorrow.

DISCIPLINE CREATES HARMONY—AT HOME AND AT WORK

Being a great father and succeeding in your career shouldn't be a constant trade-off.
It's not about doing *everything*—it's about doing the *right things* with intention and discipline.

Daily habits shape your legacy.
Structure brings peace.
And when you lead your life by design, you create balance that benefits *everyone*—including you.

Want to build better habits and lead your family with clarity and balance?
Scan the QR code or visit www.erikwestrumbook.com to begin your FREE 7-Day Fatherhood Challenge today.

Because when you lead with discipline, you gain freedom—to show up fully where it matters most.

CHAPTER 8

THE LEGACY YOU LEAVE

"A good man leaves an inheritance to his children's children."

– Proverbs 13:22

Your role as a father is not just about today—it's about the future generations that will be shaped by the choices you make right now. The influence you have on your children will ripple through time, long after you are gone.

Every father leaves a legacy. The question is, what kind will yours be?

Will your children remember you as a man who was present, disciplined, and faithful?

Will they pass down the wisdom, habits, and values you instilled in them?

Or will they struggle to define what you stood for because you never made it clear?

THE LEGACY THAT LASTS

Hockey was my first love.

From the first time I laced up my skates, I knew the game would shape me. It taught me discipline, resilience, and the relentless pursuit of excellence. It gave me teammates who became brothers, coaches who became mentors, and moments that became memories.

And for years, I thought that was my legacy.

The goals, the wins, the battles fought on the ice—I believed that was what I would be remembered for. I poured everything I had into the game, pushing my body to its limits, sacrificing time, energy, and comfort to chase something bigger than myself.

Then, one day, it was over.

The skates came off. The rink emptied. The game moved on.

And I realized something: Legacies in sports fade.

No matter how many goals I scored, no matter how many games I played, eventually, someone else would take my place. Someone younger, faster, stronger. The records would be broken. The banners would collect dust. The nameplate on my locker would be replaced with another.

It wasn't a depressing thought—it was just reality.

But as I stood at that crossroads, no longer a professional hockey player but a father, I had to ask myself:

What legacy will outlast me?

THE ETERNAL LEGACY

The answer was right in front of me.

It wasn't in a trophy case. It wasn't in highlight reels.

It was in my kids.

The way I showed up for them. The way I led them, not just in words, but in actions. The values I instilled. The lessons I taught—not just about hard work and discipline, but about character, faith, love, and perseverance.

Hockey shaped me, but fatherhood defined me.

Because long after my skates collected dust, long after the game had forgotten my name, my impact as a father would still be alive—in the way my kids treated others, in the way they pursued their dreams, in the way they carried the lessons I had taught them into their own lives.

THE REAL SCOREBOARD

I used to measure success in goals, assists, and championships.

Now, I measure success in moments.

In bedtime stories. In tough conversations. In the way my kids look to me for guidance, not just when things are easy, but when life gets hard.

Because anyone can leave a legacy in a game.

But only a father can leave a legacy in his children—one that outlasts the wins and losses, one that carries on for generations.

And that?

That's the only legacy that truly matters.

The time to intentionally craft your legacy is now.

WHAT IS A LEGACY?

Legacy isn't just about what you leave behind financially—it's about the impact you leave in the hearts and minds of your children.

Your legacy is built through:

- The values you live by – Your children will inherit your principles, integrity, and character.
- The traditions you establish – Family routines, faith practices, and rituals become lasting memories.
- The lessons you teach – How you handle adversity, relationships, and responsibility shapes their worldview.
- The love and wisdom you pass down – Your children will either be strengthened by your presence or left with gaps to fill.

A legacy is not built in a single moment—it is built in the daily choices you make as a father.

YOUR CHILDREN WILL BECOME WHO YOU ARE

Children may not always remember what you say, but they will never forget how you lived.

- If you were a man of integrity, they will carry that forward.
- If you lead with faith and discipline, they will use those lessons to guide their own lives.
- If you were intentional as a father, your children will be the same with their families.

Your legacy is not about perfection—it's about consistency. Your children don't need a perfect father; they need a father who shows up, leads with purpose, and lives in alignment with the values he teaches.

THE POWER OF TRADITIONS & VALUES

A key part of legacy is creating meaningful traditions that will outlive you. Traditions give children a sense of belonging, identity, and purpose.

Consider starting traditions such as:

- Faith practices – Family prayer, devotionals, or Sunday reflections
- Rites of passage – A father-son or father-daughter milestone event when they reach certain ages
- Character-building activities – Service projects, fitness challenges, or father-child adventures
- Annual family experiences – A camping trip, game night, or special meal that your children will pass down

These traditions reinforce values and keep your legacy alive for generations.

LESSONS YOUR CHILDREN WILL CARRY FORWARD

One of the most powerful things you can do as a father is to be intentional about what lessons you want to pass down.

Think about the key lessons you want your children to carry forward into adulthood.

1. The Power of Discipline & Hard Work

Success is built on daily habits, not just big moments.

Teach your children that hard work, discipline, and consistency lead to freedom.

2. Faith as a Foundation

God will always be your anchor in life's storms.

Help them understand that faith is the foundation of a purpose-driven life.

3. The Importance of Integrity

Your character is the only thing no one can take from you.

Instill the principle that doing the right thing is always worth it, even when no one is watching.

4. Strength in Resilience

You don't fail when you fall—you fail when you quit.

Show them that setbacks are opportunities to grow and become stronger.

5. The Value of Relationships & Family

Your family is your first team—treat them with love, respect, and loyalty.

Model how to be a great husband, father, and friend.

Every lesson you live out is a piece of your legacy.

HOW TO BE REMEMBERED AS A FATHER

At the end of your life, your children won't care how much money you made, how many hours you worked, or how many awards you received.

They will remember:

- The times you were there when they needed you.
- The values you lived by and passed down.
- The way you made them feel loved, supported, and encouraged.

Your presence, leadership, and example will become the foundation of their lives.

Are you building a legacy worth remembering?

FINAL THOUGHT: YOUR LEGACY STARTS NOW

Fatherhood is not about perfection—it's about intention.

The decisions you make today are shaping your children's future, their character, and the values they will pass down to their own families.

You are writing your legacy right now.

The question is: What story will it tell?

THE FATHERHOOD *by Design* GAME PLAN

Write a Legacy Letter

Take a few quiet moments to write a letter to your child.

Include:

- A few key lessons you want them to remember
- The values you hope they live by
- The love, pride, and belief you have in them

You can give it to them now—or save it for a milestone moment.

Because your words may one day become their anchor.

THE LEGACY YOU LEAVE STARTS TODAY

Your legacy isn't built someday—it's built daily, in the quiet moments, the consistent choices, and the way you lead your family.

It's not about what you leave *for* your children…
It's about what you leave *in* them—faith, strength, discipline, and love.

Every moment you show up with purpose, you're writing the story they'll remember.

Ready to become the father your children will thank you for?
Scan the QR code or visit www.erikwestrumbook.com to access your FREE 7-Day Fatherhood Challenge today.

Because the greatest legacy you leave won't be your success—it'll be your *example.*

CONCLUSION

YOUR FATHERHOOD GAME PLAN

"It is easier to build strong children than to repair broken men."

– Frederick Douglass

Embarking on the journey of fatherhood can feel like navigating an uncharted wilderness. The pressure to leave a lasting legacy while being the perfect parent can be overwhelming. However, the secret to successful parenting isn't found in striving for perfection, but in embracing a structured approach to nurturing and engaging relationships with our children. This final chapter offers fathers a practical, manageable plan, designed to strengthen your fatherly presence and deepen your connection with your children.

The framework outlined here is not just about checking boxes; it's about initiating deep, meaningful change. It's about setting realistic goals, reflecting on daily interactions, and continuously adapting strategies to meet the ever-evolving challenges of parenthood. Through this structured approach, you will learn how to alleviate the stress associated with legacy-building and focus more on the moments that truly matter.

FATHERHOOD: THE ULTIMATE GAME PLAN

Every athlete knows that success doesn't happen by accident.

Before every game, before every season, there's a game plan—a strategy designed to maximize strengths, minimize weaknesses, and prepare for whatever challenges lie ahead. Without a game plan, even the most talented team will stumble. They'll play reactively instead of proactively. They'll make mistakes they could have avoided.

Fatherhood is no different.

Just like in sports, you don't win as a dad by winging it.

THE PRE-GAME STRATEGY: DEFINING THE VISION

Before a team steps onto the ice, onto the field, or into the arena, the coach sits them down and lays out the game plan.

- What's our goal?
- What's our strategy?
- What do we need to focus on to succeed?

As a father, if you don't define what success looks like for your family, how will you know if you're leading well?

- What values do I want to instill in my kids?
- What kind of role model do I want to be?

- What habits, disciplines, and lessons do I need to reinforce every single day?

If you don't have a vision, fatherhood becomes reactive instead of intentional. You'll spend your time responding to problems instead of preparing your kids for life's challenges.

TRAINING CAMP: LEADING BY EXAMPLE

Every great athlete understands that practice makes perfect. Game plans mean nothing if you don't put in the work.

In hockey, you can't tell your team to be disciplined if you show up late to practice. You can't demand accountability if you aren't holding yourself accountable. Your actions set the tone for how your team responds.

The same is true in fatherhood.

I can't expect my kids to be disciplined if I'm inconsistent. I can't expect them to be kind if I'm short-tempered. I can't tell them to be strong in their faith if they never see me pray, read the Bible, or live out what I preach.

Just like in sports, fatherhood is about leading by example.

Your kids are watching how you handle adversity, how you treat people, how you respond to failure. You set the standard—not by what you say, but by how you live.

GAME DAY: NAVIGATING THE UNEXPECTED

No matter how much you prepare, no game ever goes exactly as planned.

An opponent might surprise you with a new strategy. A referee might make a bad call. A key player might get injured. That's why great coaches adjust on the fly—they don't throw out the game plan, but they adapt as needed.

Parenting is the same way.

You can have all the best intentions, all the structure in the world, but life will throw unexpected challenges at you.

- Your kids will struggle in ways you never anticipated.
- You'll face moments of failure, doubt, and frustration.
- Some days, you'll feel like you're winning. Other days, you'll feel like you're failing.

But just like in sports, sticking to your core principles is what keeps you on track.

The key is consistency. Staying steady when things get tough. Showing up when you don't feel like it. Encouraging your kids even when you're exhausted. Teaching them how to adapt without abandoning what matters most.

POST-GAME REFLECTION: LEARNING FROM MISTAKES

After every game, a coach sits down with the team to review what went well and what didn't. They study film, analyze mistakes, and make adjustments for the next game.

That's exactly how fatherhood works.

I've made plenty of mistakes. There have been times I wasn't present enough, times I lost my patience, times I focused more on work than my family. But just like in sports, the key is to reflect, learn, and adjust.

I won't always get it right—but I can always get better.

THE CHAMPIONSHIP MINDSET: PLAYING THE LONG GAME

In sports, the ultimate goal isn't just to win a single game—it's to build a championship team. That takes long-term vision, daily discipline, and relentless effort.

Fatherhood is the same.

It's not about having one great moment—it's about showing up consistently. Day after day. Season after season. Year after year—until your kids are not only grown but fully prepared for life on their own.

And here's the truth: fatherhood doesn't end when your kids leave the house.

Your role may change, but your influence doesn't disappear.

The strong relationships you build with your children now—through presence, trust, discipline, and love—lay the foundation for a lifelong connection. One that extends into their adulthood, their challenges, their families, and even their own fatherhood journeys one day.

This is the long game.

It's about preparing them to win at life, not just survive it.

Because being a great father isn't about being perfect.

It's about having a game plan, sticking to your principles, and leading with love, discipline, and purpose—no matter what challenges come your way.

That's why I've broken this transformative fatherhood journey into three key steps:

1. Developing a structured plan
2. Setting achievable goals
3. Reflecting and adapting over time

Each step builds upon the last—creating a powerful rhythm of intentional growth. Not just for a few weeks, or during the early years, but throughout your lifetime as a father.

This is your legacy. This is your team.

Play the long game—and play it well.

DEVELOPING A STRUCTURED PLAN

The first step is all about creating a blueprint for daily engagement with your children. This isn't about overhauling your entire life, but integrating small, impactful interactions into your existing routine. These moments are tailored to fit naturally into your day, so they become sustainable practices rather than additional tasks on your to-do list.

SETTING ACHIEVABLE GOALS

Next, we focus on setting goals that serve as the milestones for this journey. These aren't just any goals; they are carefully thought-out objectives aimed at enhancing specific aspects of your relationship with your children. Whether it's improving communication, increasing quality time spent together, or teaching new skills, these goals are designed to bring noticeable improvements in family dynamics.

REFLECTING AND ADAPTING

The final step is perhaps the most crucial, and that is reflection. This stage encourages you to look back at what has been accomplished, what worked well, and what could be improved. Reflection provides the insights needed to adapt your strategies and continue growing as an impactful father. It's about learning from every step of the journey and using that knowledge to better yourself and your relationship with your children.

As we approach the conclusion of our journey together, remember that these steps are only the beginning of what will be an ongoing adventure in disciplined, connected parenting. The practices you establish now lay the groundwork for the lifelong bond you are building with your children.

By embracing this structured approach to fatherhood, you'll find that managing day-to-day parenting responsibilities becomes less daunting and more rewarding. You'll discover that being present goes beyond simply being there physically; it's about engaging emotionally and intellectually with your children in ways that leave a lasting impact.

So, let's move forward with confidence, knowing that each small step we take is shaping a legacy of love, guidance, and support, which is a true testament to disciplined, connected parenting.

PART ONE: DEVELOPING A STRUCTURED PLAN

Fatherhood demands more than just being physically present. It requires an active, engaged approach that fosters deep connections. It is vital to begin with a structured plan. This plan acts like a blueprint for a house; it outlines the foundation upon which strong relationships are built. It's about being there, truly listening and engaging, whether it's during a hockey game or a school play.

Imagine fatherhood as a garden. Your presence is the water and sunlight needed to nourish this garden. Without consistent care, the garden won't thrive. This analogy underscores the necessity of a structured approach to fatherly engagement—it's not sporadic, but regular and deliberate, ensuring that each interaction with your child is meaningful.

Creating this structured plan involves setting specific times for activities, being fully present during these moments, and minimizing distractions. It's about quality over quantity. Engaging in activities that both you and your child enjoy can significantly enhance the quality of the time spent together. This could be as simple as reading a book every night or as involved as a weekly adventure outdoors.

The effectiveness of this approach lies in its routine nature. Children thrive on consistency, and a reliable schedule of engagement helps them feel secure and valued. This consistency also helps fathers by removing the guesswork out of when and how they'll interact with their children, making it easier to balance other responsibilities.

Ultimately, developing a structured plan to enhance fatherly presence and engagement is about creating consistent, quality interactions that foster a secure, supportive relationship with your children.

PART TWO: SETTING ACHIEVABLE GOALS

Meaningful goal setting in fatherhood transforms good intentions into actionable steps. It's about identifying what tangible outcomes you want from your relationship with your child and setting up steps to achieve these outcomes. For example, if your goal is to improve communication with your teenager, specific aims might include dedicating 15 minutes each day to talk about anything they're interested in.

Why set goals? Goals give you a target, a point on the horizon to aim for. They convert unclear desires into concrete paths to follow. Each goal acts as a checkpoint in the journey of fatherhood, helping you gauge your progress and stay on track.

Goals should be SMART: Specific, Measurable, Attainable, Relevant, and Time-bound. This framework ensures that your objectives are distinct and achievable, providing a clear pathway rather than a vague ambition. For instance, rather than a broad goal like "spend more time with my child," a SMART goal would be "spend 30 minutes each day playing or talking with my child."

The process of achieving these goals should be flexible. Life is unpredictable, and the needs of your children will change as they grow. Adapting your methods and sometimes even your goals ensures that you remain responsive to your children's development.

Reflecting on these goals regularly to assess whether they are still relevant and whether you are on track is also crucial. This reflection can be as simple as a weekly review of what went well and what could be better. It's about continuous improvement rather than rigid adherence to a plan.

Could setting clear, achievable goals be the key to building lasting and fulfilling relationships with your children? I genuinely believe it is.

PART THREE: REFLECTING AND ADAPTING FATHERHOOD STRATEGIES

Embracing change and adaptation in fatherhood is essential for growth. The Fatherhood Transformation Framework is designed to guide fathers through a structured process of enhancement in their roles. This framework is broken down into five phases: reflection, goal setting, action planning, implementation, and review.

Reflection

The journey begins with reflection. This phase is about understanding where you currently stand in your relationship with your children. What are your strengths? Where could you improve? This could involve writing down your thoughts, feelings, and experiences in a journal or discussing them with a partner or a friend. Reflection sets the stage for effective goal setting by providing a clear picture of what needs to change. This is a recalibration of revisiting your initial plan and goals to see where you are and where you want to be in order to readjust as needed.

Goal Setting

Next is the goal-setting phase. Here, fathers define what they want to achieve based on their reflections. Remember to set goals with the SMART criteria to ensure they are clear and reachable within the desired timeframe. This phase turns introspection into action by outlining what fathers hope to accomplish after reflecting on what is working and what needs to be adjusted.

Action Planning

With goals in place, the next step is to develop a detailed action plan. This plan breaks down each goal into smaller, manageable tasks, specifying when and how these tasks will be accomplished. It's a blueprint that guides fathers on the daily, weekly, and monthly actions needed to reach their goals. This is an extension of your structured plan.

Implementation

The implementation phase is where plans are put into action. This is the test of commitment and adaptability, as real-life challenges may require fathers to adjust their plans. Staying flexible and focused during this phase is crucial for maintaining progress towards goals, taking one step at a time.

Review

Finally, the review phase allows fathers to evaluate their progress at the end of the desired timeline. It's a time to celebrate successes, learn from setbacks, and, if necessary, adjust goals and strategies moving forward. This phase closes the loop of the cycle but also opens it up for continued growth and development.

This structured approach not only helps fathers become more present and engaged, but also ensures they adapt to the changing dynamics of their relationship with their children, thereby continually refining their approach to fatherhood.

Over the period of your life, you'll embark on a transformative journey, utilizing a structured approach to enhance your role as a father. Through setting clear goals and reflecting on your progress, you'll begin to see tangible improvements in your family dynamics and your connection with your children. This process isn't just about being present; it's about being engaged and intentional in every interaction with your family.

By developing a structured plan, you have addressed the overwhelming feeling that often accompanies the desire to be a perfect father. Remember, perfection in parenting is unattainable, but improvement is always within reach. Your commitment to this plan shows your dedication not only to your own growth, but also to the well-being and development of your children.

Reflecting on your progress is crucial. It allows you to see what strategies are working and what might need adjustment. This ongoing cycle of action, evaluation, and adaptation is the cornerstone of disciplined, connected parenting. It's what turns short-term changes into lasting legacies.

As you move forward, keep setting achievable and meaningful goals. These should continue to challenge you, but also be realistic enough to keep you motivated. Celebrate the victories, no matter how small, and learn from the setbacks without letting them define your journey.

Remember, the essence of impactful fatherhood lies in everyday moments. It's found in the morning hugs, the bedtime stories, and the supportive conversations. Each day presents a new opportunity to strengthen these bonds and reinforce the values you wish to instill in your children.

This book has equipped you with the tools to not only face the challenges of fatherhood, but to thrive amidst them. By embracing the principles of disciplined, connected parenting, you're setting a foundation that will support your children's growth into confident, resilient individuals.

Keep leveraging your "Fatherhood Game Plan," staying true to your values, and adjusting your strategies as needed. The roadmap you create and follow is just the beginning. Continue to cultivate discipline, lead by example, and foster strong connections. Your journey as an impactful father doesn't end here—it evolves.

Your dedication to this path is a powerful testament to the love you have for your children and your commitment to their future. As you forge ahead, remember that every day brings a new chance to shape your legacy—a legacy of love, strength, and connection. Here's to continuing your journey with confidence, purpose, and joy.

THE PLAN IS IN YOUR HANDS—NOW IT'S TIME TO LEAD

You've read the principles.
You've seen the steps.
You've got the framework to lead with purpose.

But knowledge alone doesn't build strong families—action does.

Your *Fatherhood by Design Game Plan* isn't just a set of ideas—it's a *call to lead, love, and live with intention.*

Don't just put this book down—pick up the responsibility. Scan the QR code or visit www.erikwestrumbook.com to activate your FREE 7-Day Fatherhood Challenge and begin applying what you've learned *today*.

Because your kids don't need a perfect father…
They need a present, intentional one—starting now.

EPILOGUE

THE JOURNEY FORWARD

"To be successful at anything, the truth is you don't have to be special. You just have to be what most people aren't: consistent, determined, and willing to work for it."

– Tom Brady

SEALING YOUR LEGACY WITH INTENTION AND ACTION

As we wrap up our time together, it's essential to reflect on the transformative journey you've embarked upon. This book was crafted not just as a guide but as a companion in your quest to redefine fatherhood for yourself and your children. Through its pages, we've explored the profound impact of disciplined, connected parenting and how it shapes the legacy you leave behind.

The practical applications of the strategies discussed are vast and tailored to slip seamlessly into your daily life. Whether it's through setting clear, actionable goals, engaging in meaningful conversations with your children, or leading by example in every aspect of your life, these tools are designed to elevate your parenting approach. Implementing these practices will not only strengthen your relationship with your children, but also enrich your personal growth and fulfillment as a father.

We've revisited several key concepts throughout our journey—presence, purpose, and discipline. Each of these pillars is crucial in building a strong foundation for both personal and parental success. By consistently applying these principles, you can expect to see a remarkable transformation not only in your children, but in yourself as well.

To truly benefit from this book, I encourage you to take deliberate steps towards integrating these insights into your daily routines. Reflect on the exercises provided, revisit your "Fatherhood Game Plan" regularly, and remain open to adjusting your strategies as you grow alongside your children.

EMBRACING IMPERFECTION AND CONTINUOUS LEARNING

It's important to acknowledge that the path to becoming an impactful father is not short of challenges. There may be days when things don't go as planned or when doubts creep in—this is normal. What matters most is your commitment to persevere and learn from each experience.

The landscape of fatherhood is ever evolving, and thus, continuous learning is key. I invite you to stay curious about new parenting methods, seek advice from fellow fathers, and perhaps most importantly, keep the lines of communication open with your family. They are not just the beneficiaries of your growth, but also valuable contributors to it.

FROM SELFISH TO SELFLESS: THE TRANSFORMATION THAT DEFINED MY FATHERHOOD

Looking back, I see the man I used to be.

I was driven, ambitious, determined to succeed—but I was also self-centered. I told myself that my long hours, my networking, my endless pursuit of success were all for my family. That providing for them financially was the ultimate measure of a great father.

But I missed the most important part.

I gave them everything except the one thing they needed most—me.

I was physically present but emotionally absent. I was showing up when it was convenient, but not when it mattered. I was chasing the things that filled my bucket, while leaving theirs empty.

THE BREAKING POINT

I've told stories throughout this book—of how I got cut from the A hockey team and had to learn mental toughness, of how I spent nights in scrubs instead of leading my family in faith, of how I poured into coaching other kids while neglecting my own, of how I was stuck in the trap of workaholism, failing to balance my priorities.

But all of those lessons led me to one undeniable truth:

Fatherhood is not about me.

It's about them.

It's about being a leader in my home, not just in my career. It's about serving my wife and kids, not expecting them to accommodate my schedule, my needs, my ambitions.

It's about stepping up every single day—not just when I feel like it, not just when it's convenient, but when it's needed.

HOW I SHOW UP NOW

The difference between the father I was and the father I am today is simple: I lead with intention.

Now, when I wake up, the first thing I do isn't check emails or think about work. I start my day with prayer, reading the Bible, and working out—because if I'm not strong in faith, in mind, and in body, how can I expect to lead my family well?

I've learned that structure creates freedom. My family knows that when I'm working, I'm locked in. But when I'm home, I'm fully present. Phones down. Eyes up. Engaged in real conversations, not just "How was your day?" surface-level talk.

I no longer just tell my kids to be disciplined—I show them. They see me waking up early. They see me setting goals. They see me following through on commitments. Because kids don't learn from what you say, they learn from what you do.

I no longer just talk about faith—I lead with it. I pray with my kids. I read the Bible with them. I show them that faith isn't a Sunday routine, but a way of life. I teach them that being a man isn't about how much money you make or how tough you act, but about how well you serve.

I no longer just provide financially—I provide emotionally. I show up for my wife, not just as a husband but as a partner. I listen. I support. I invest in our marriage because I know that the way I treat her is the way my kids will one day treat their own spouses.

A THOUGHT LEADER FOR FATHERS

I don't just talk about these principles in my own home—I share them with fathers everywhere.

I coach, I mentor, I lead. I help men step into their roles as intentional fathers, leaders, and husbands. I teach them what I had to learn the hard way—that success at work means nothing if you're failing at home.

I challenge fathers to be all in—not just in their careers, not just in their hobbies, but in the most important calling they will ever have: in raising the next generation.

This is why I wrote this book.

Not to pat myself on the back. Not to pretend I have all the answers.

But to show that transformation is possible.

That no matter where you are today—whether you're distracted, disconnected, inconsistent, or lost—you can change the narrative.

You can go from selfish to selfless.

You can lead your family with strength, faith, and intention.

And when your kids look back one day, they won't remember the money you made, the deals you closed, or the trophies on your shelf.

They'll remember the father you were.

And that—that's the legacy that lasts forever.

TAKE ACTION: YOUR LEGACY AWAITS

Now is the time to step forward with confidence and determination. Harness the strategies you've learned; let them guide you toward becoming the father you aspire to be—one who leads with strength, nurtures with wisdom, and loves with depth.

As you continue on this path, remember that every small effort contributes significantly to the tapestry of your children's futures. You have the power to mold those precious lives through every action you take and every word you speak.

FINAL THOUGHTS: A CALL TO LEAD BY EXAMPLE

In closing, let me leave you with this thought: The essence of impactful fatherhood lies not in perfection, but in presence. Every moment spent engaged in the betterment of yourself and your relationship with your children is a step toward a lasting legacy—a legacy of love, strength, and integrity.

"Children are not a distraction from more important work. They are the most important work." - C.S. Lewis

Let this powerful reminder steer you back whenever you find yourself at a crossroads or when fatigue sets in. Remember why you started this journey—your children deserve the best version of "you" that there can be.

The question is: are you willing to be that father?

THE JOURNEY FORWARD STARTS NOW

Fatherhood isn't a destination—it's a daily journey.

Some days you'll feel strong. Other days, uncertain.
But every step you take in love, in discipline, and in faith moves your family forward.

You've been equipped with tools, truth, and a clear vision.
Now it's time to walk it out—with courage, with consistency, and by design.

Ready to take the next step on your journey?
Scan the QR code or visit www.erikwestrumbook.com to access your FREE 7-Day Fatherhood Challenge and continue growing as the father you were created to be.

The future of your family is shaped by what you choose to do today.
Lead boldly. Love intentionally. Keep moving forward.

7-DAY FATHERHOOD *by Design* CHALLENGE

Reading this book is a great start, but true transformation happens through action.

The next step? Commit to the 7-Day Fatherhood by Design Challenge—a focused, intentional plan to help you implement the principles you've learned in this book and deepen your connection with your children.

This challenge isn't about perfection or adding more to your plate—it's about small, powerful actions that create lasting impact. Each day will focus on a key area of intentional fatherhood, giving you practical steps to lead with discipline, connection, and purpose.

HOW IT WORKS

Each day, you'll have one simple, actionable challenge.

These small, intentional steps will build consistency and momentum.

At the end of the week, you'll feel more engaged, present, and confident as a father.

Day 1: The Power of Presence – "Phone Down, Eyes Up"

Action Step: For at least 30 minutes today, put your phone away, turn off distractions, and be fully present with your child. Whether it's talking, playing, or just listening, give them your undivided attention.

Why? Your presence is the greatest gift you can give. Small moments create lasting memories.

Day 2: Words of Life – "Speak Life into Your Child"

Action Step: Today, intentionally affirm and encourage your child. Tell them something specific you admire about them, like their kindness, effort, or creativity.

Why? A father's words shape a child's self-esteem, confidence, and belief in themselves.

Day 3: Lead with Love – "Apologize or Acknowledge"

Action Step: Reflect on any recent moment when you may have been short-tempered, distracted, or misunderstood your child. If needed, apologize, or acknowledge it with them. If not, simply share a meaningful lesson about life or fatherhood with them today.

Why? Great fathers lead with humility and openness, teaching their kids the power of reflection and repair.

Day 4: Create a Connection Ritual – "One-on-One Time"

Action Step: Plan a short but meaningful one-on-one activity with each of your children. It could be a walk, playing a game, reading a book together, or sharing a meal—something that fosters connection.

Why? Consistent quality time strengthens the father-child bond, even in small increments.

Day 5: Build a Legacy – "Write a Letter to Your Child"

Action Step: Write your child a heartfelt letter or note, sharing:

What you love about them

Your hopes for their future

A lesson you want them to remember

You can give it to them now or save it for the future. This can be an extension of the exercise you did in Chapter 8 or a new letter.

Why? Your words today can become their anchor in the future.

Day 6: Teach & Inspire – "Share a Life Lesson"

Action Step: Tell your child a story from your life that teaches a lesson. Maybe it's about perseverance, kindness, mistakes, or resilience. Let them see your journey and the wisdom you've gained.

Why? Children learn best from stories and personal experiences, not just lectures.

Day 7: Set an Intention – "How Will You Show Up Going Forward?"

Action Step: Reflect on the past six days. What felt most meaningful? Choose one habit you will continue doing regularly and write it down. Share it with your child if you'd like!

Why? Growth isn't about doing everything at once, but committing to small, lasting improvements.

YOUR LEGACY BEGINS TODAY

Once you've completed the 7-Day Fatherhood by Design Challenge, it will only be the beginning.

Your kids don't need you to be perfect—they need you to be intentional, present, and committed to growth.

So, ask yourself:

- What kind of father do you want to be?
- What values will you pass on?
- What legacy will your children carry forward?

Now go lead your family with purpose. Because the impact you make isn't measured in moments of recognition, but in the quiet consistency of your love, discipline, and presence.

Lead with purpose. Live with conviction. Love without limits.

Your family is watching. Your legacy is unfolding.

"Be on guard; stand firm in the faith; be courageous; be strong. Do everything in love." – 1 Corinthians 16:13-14

Now go—be the father your children will always remember.

Join the Fatherhood by Design Community to continue learning, growing, and connecting with like-minded fathers on this journey.

YOU DON'T HAVE TO DO THIS ALONE

Fatherhood is one of the most important—and most challenging—roles you'll ever carry.
But you weren't meant to walk this road alone.

Join the Fatherhood by Design Community to keep learning, growing, and connecting with like-minded fathers who are committed to leading with purpose.

Inside, you'll find:
✓ Real conversations
✓ Practical tools
✓ Encouragement for your journey
✓ Brotherhood that builds you up

Scan the QR code or visit www.erikwestrumbook.com to join today.

Because when strong fathers come together, families—and legacies—are transformed.

Your kids don't need a perfect father, they need a present, intentional one-starting now.

ABOUT THE AUTHOR

Erik Westrum is a devoted husband, father, leadership coach, and former professional hockey player who has dedicated his life to helping men lead with intention and purpose. Drawing from his experiences in elite sports, business leadership, and personal growth, Erik equips fathers with the tools to cultivate strong relationships, instill discipline, and leave a lasting legacy for their children.

As the founder of *Fatherhood by Design*, Erik mentors men to step up as leaders in their homes and communities, empowering them to become the fathers their children need. His transformational coaching programs and speaking engagements inspire men worldwide to embrace their role with confidence and clarity.

Beyond his work in fatherhood and leadership, Erik is passionate about mental health awareness. Through his charity, he provides resources and support to help fathers, and their children, navigate life's challenges, lead by example, and build a strong foundation of emotional resilience. His mission is to ensure that no father—or child—has to face struggles alone.

When he's not coaching or writing, Erik enjoys quality time with his family, pushing his limits through endurance training, and living each day with purpose. He's passionate about helping others grow through intentional fatherhood, personal discipline, and strong leadership. Erik believes that small, consistent actions—done daily—can create meaningful, lasting impact. His mission is to help fathers lead by example and leave a legacy that matters.

www.ingramcontent.com/pod-product-compliance
Lightning Source LLC
Chambersburg PA
CBHW060324050426
42449CB00011B/2641

* 9 7 8 1 9 6 7 7 3 2 0 4 3 *